The Devil and Michael Scot

PREVIOUS BOOKS OF POETRY: *THE CHAGALL WINNOCKS AND PARAPETS AND LABYRINTHS*

The wandering scholar is a great European tradition and Scotland has had her share, poets, singers, the restless and endlessly curious, travelling workers in literature, language and the arts. Among the most distinctive riches yielded by this tradition, Tom Hubbard's poems are evocative encounters with places, people, political and personal states, that range across Europe and history, centred in his own Scottish sensibility, but receptive to, exploring and describing, different nations, artists and cultures. Particular accounts of engagement with others indicate matters of value and illumination, not least the stained-glass windows of Marc Chagall and the symphonies of Carl Nielsen. These poems are day-books of travel and meditation, records of what art can do, the good of all the arts, through all the galleries and balconies of Europe. They are arcades of wonder.

– ALAN RIACH, poet and Professor of Scottish
Literature at the University of Glasgow

THE FLECHITORIUM:

The Flechitorium is a delicious Fife broth or even Langtoun bouillabaisse if you prefer, with its many hints and references to other literary cuisines beyond Fife and Scotland. At times it is funny, at others serious, it is always humane in its span of concerns from bawdy to spiritual yet the poems are crafted to address and engage intellectually as well as emotionally. Whether supped with short or lang spuin it will satisfy all tastes.

– WILLIAM HERSHAW,
makar and musician,
Lochgelly

The Devil and Michael Scot

A Gallimaufry of Fife and Beyond

Tom Hubbard

GRACE NOTE PUBLICATIONS

The Devil and Michael Scot
A Gallimaufry of Fife and Beyond
This edition published 2020 by
Grace Note Publications C.I.C.
Grange of Locherlour,
Ochtertyre, PH7 4JS,
Scotland

books@gracenotereading.co.uk

ISBN 978-1-913162-10-8

First published in 2020

With images by the author

A catalogue record for this book is available
from the British Library

TO THE MEMORY OF
DUNCAN AND MARGARET GLEN

CONTENTS

Foreword
1

1. Introduction
3

2. A Testament of Fife – First Part.
Mugdrum to Balcomie
5

3. Clean Pride and Mucky pride.
Parochialism versus Provincialism
9

4. A Testament of Fife – Second Part.
Monimail to Craigtoun
11

5. Bleak Fertility:
Robert Louis Stevenson and Fife
12

6. A Testament of Fife – Third Part.
Cupar to Lower Largo
22

7. Herman Melville,
Fife and *Moby-Dick*
24

8. A Testament of Fife – Fourth Part.
Methil to the Caves and Abandoned Pits
43

9. Walkin in Fife:
Duncan Glen, Markinch and Points North
45

10. A Testament of Fife – Fifth Part.
Ravenscraig to Kirkcaldy
49

11. Adam Smith's 'Sympathy' Symphony
51

12. The Devil and Michael Scot, a play
55

13. A Testament of Fife – Sixth Part.
Kinghorn to Hawkcraig
112

14. Fife's Culture, Past and Present:
Joe Corrie (1894-1968) and the Bowhill Players
115

15. Hauf a Kilt in Kelty
121

16. A Testament of Fife - Seventh Part.
Dunfermline
123

17. No new Stories: Robert Henrysoun and
Alexander Pushkin
128

18. A Testament of Fife – Eighth Part.
Inverkeithing via Benarty to Kincardine
131

19. Notes
133

20. Glossary / Wordleet
145

21. About the Author
151

FOREWORD

An old man is climbing the steep hill from the Forth to the City of Edinburgh, carrying his lum hat. High Victorian days. Behind and below him are familiar locals, fishwives with their creels, tough bargainers long before Adam Smith knew them. There are ships in the Firth, even a steamer or two, and Tom Hubbard's Kirkcaldy on the far shore - the 'Kinrick' of Fife which appropriately houses this most cosmopolitan of writers. For the librarian – we'll come to that - knows the fascination and ever-exfoliating world of fact and random narrative, and that's difficult to square with the drama.

The old man, Dr Morison, has just conjured good out of tragedy. The painter Richard Dadd 'The Fairy Feller' had, during a depressive fit, stabbed his father to death, and would spend the rest of his life in an asylum, but he could still paint and his doctor enabled him to continue. Morison furnished the landscape at second hand: the fishwives, meadows and buildings are from the 'calotypes' of the first photographs: the slides of Adamson and Hill. This is the sort of complicated tale that many librarians love, and through their care and hard work, open up to the public.

This is what makes Tom Hubbard such a rewarding guide: a man steeped in the places and tales of the Kinrick who doesn't get run over by them, rather he manages to unfold fresh visions, partly because - as cosmopolitan traveller and translator, all human effort lies before him. Maybe refracted through the changing seas before the folk of the lang toun of Kirkcaldy - from douce Adam Smith to danger-woman Mary Shelley, who sometimes stayed at nearby Balgonie with the Stuart family. Their son David would start the University Extension movement, forerunner of nearby Jennie Lee's Open University.

What better choice than Tom could there have been to guide the Scottish Poetry Library, when it opened off Edinburgh's High Street and Canongate? Its ethos 'Open the doors and begin!' was planted: that trumpet-like flourish ends Edwin Morgan's greeting to the new Parliament. This is the business of the librarian which should - we hope - lie behind our academies, in the stored reserves of our culture.

Michael Scot may or may not be buried in Melrose; the ruin has a medieval image there of him in Arab costume, and I like to think that the 'Great Michael' - early Renaissance Scotland's capital ship, nodded to the firepower of the man who took the Greek language from its Arab custodians like the great Averroës, and restored it to the Europe of the northern Master. Salve!

CHRISTOPHER HARVIE

A native of Motherwell who grew up in the Borders, Christopher Harvie is Emeritus Professor of British and Irish Studies at the University of Tübingen in Germany, and the author of many books. From 2007 to 2011 he was a Scottish National Party Member of the Scottish Parliament for Mid Scotland and Fife.

1. INTRODUCTION

This book offers you a virtual tour of much of Fife, mainly of its 'fringe of gold', so it could serve as an idiosyncratic guide to the Coastal Path and more. It starts just west of Newburgh at the border with Perthshire and ends at the Kincardine Bridge, with substantial forays inland.

The centre-piece, which provides the title of our gallimaufry, is a play based on the vicissitudes of Michael Scot of Balwearie, the medieval wizard / scientist / polymath famous in both legend and history, and centering on his pact with the devil. There's an earlier Fife drama, though, about our local hero. In 2016 there appeared *Michael: a Ballad Play in Scots* by my fellow-makar and close friend William Hershaw, and I was honoured to be called on to act several parts for a recording made by his son David. Willie told me that I had made Michael's sometime gaffer, Frederick King of Sicily and Hohenzollern Emperor, sound like a Bond villain; someone else said that my Saturn, that stern judge in the play's Epilogue, came across as an Aberdonian sergeant-major. It was all great fun and I look forward to the recording's availability to the public on the Scotsoun label.

Willie and I made our own demonic pact to offer two very different takes on the Michael material, and he was happy for my obsession with the Faust legend to run riot through my own version. So here it is in the following pages.

The present book could act as a companion to my previous offerings, *Slavonic Dances* and *The Flechitorium*, both published by Grace Notes Publications. Both these books view Fife in markedly European and world contexts; as its title suggests, *Slavonic Dances* looks east, and from viewpoints within Fife. In the present book, there are many references to Russia and its literature, including translations from that great poet of Scottish – and Fife – ancestry, Mikhaïl Lermontov. You'll come across a seemingly odd pairing of Robert Henrysoun, Dunfermline's makar 'of European reputation' (as Dickens's Mrs Bayham Badger would put it) and Alexander Pushkin. Even more bizarre, possibly, is Adam Smith presented here as a sort of Mozart living beyond the age of 35. Don't blame me: at Glasgow University there's a statue of 'the father of economics', arm outstretched, as if he were conducting a symphony.

TOM HUBBARD
September 2019

2. A TESTAMENT OF FIFE –
FIRST PART.
MUGDRUM TO BALCOMIE

Mugdrum, Newburgh, Ormiston Hill,
Macduff's Cross: its sometime sanctuary,
Yet present prospect, loved by Walter Scott
For span of mountain-scape, from glen to sea,

By confluence of the Earn and the Tay
And a European beauty. Stones of Lindores,
Mark once-devotional space: silent the bells
That summoned shivering pilgrims to those shores.

Dunbog, Hazelton Walls, to Balmerino –
Its centuries of Spanish chestnut-tree
Spread darkly here in the late autumn sun,
I knew as young fella and now as elderly.

Wormit, Pickletillum, Tentsmuir;
Frail folk envy that forests endure –
The mediocre of privileged birth
Insist on dominion over this earth:
At the top table they smirk as they sup,
Intent on buggering everything up.

St Andrews, where the rush of water on stone
Attracts new growing minds, who from a notion
Arrive at ripe analysis, the zone
To assess such 'such interaction of land, and ocean,

For all is flowing, blending: touch in one place,
And it resonates remotely': that's Zossima
In *The Brothers Karamazov*. Here's his space,
In the Byre Theatre, for the young to play

The part of the old monk. Far to the east,
There's another stage, and another Russian's call
To the actors to allow him there to rest
From past stramash, from promise then downfall,

The public man no longer public
And newly-widowed, with his calm request
To sing to them, spontaneous, unslick,
Such loved lines of their country and its soul:

> I gang my lane, ootby towart the gate,
> The flinty wey fair glisters through the haar;
> The muirland harks ti God. The nicht is quate.
> Nou is the time when star collogues wi star.

> I see an unco glamourie in heiven!
> The yird is sleepin in a blae-like sheen ...
> Why suid I feel sic pyne, sic tire o leevin?
> Dae I wait fir ocht? Or rue the ill that's been?

> I claim nae mair frae life, naethin ava,
> I dinna hae regrets fir aa my past.
> I lang fir freedom, and fir peace anaa;
> I'd seek oblivion, win my sleep at last.

> Yit no wi the cauld muilderin o the lair:
> Raither a kind repose when I depairt,

The life-force still within me evermair,
Wi the ayebydin rhythm o the hairt.

That day and nicht, wi sic tones as please,
Sae sweet a voice wad lull me bi its chant;
And the aik-tree's brainches, darkly emerant,
Wad bend and reestle ower me at my ease.

From the Russian of Mikhaïl Lermontov (1814-41)

Aloof from every human mess,
The Rock and Spindle at Kinkell Ness,

Eldritch as the Den at Dunino
Where we ponder in vain. – And yet Cambo,

Welcoming forest in the spring,
White clustered on green, first burgeoning.

Balcomie's stones of far imagining,
Its halls paced by its high exalted folk;
Silence of centuries for those who sing
Of long displacement, who seek light through smoke,

Smoke, the unknowing of our evanescence;
So the young Russian, stirred by Walter Scott,
Strove for his own elusive coalescence,
Till death approached, unmasked, and then – the
    shot.

  Why am I not that raven of the steppe,
  Cawing defiantly there above me?
  I would fly to the fogs of the far west,

The castle's stones precipitous to the sea.
On my ancestral walls the proud shield:
The sword of my clan:
With but my wing I'd brush off the dust
For those stern splendours to be revealed.
From the minstrels' hall, I'd strum the harp
With these proud feathers; down and deep
Into the vaults, such music surely can
Call up the troubled knight from bitter sleep.
But my own dreams are idle. Alps and oceans
Bar all my claims: I breathe cold, alien air.
Why am I not a raven of the steppe?
Here was I born: my soul belongs elsewhere ...

From the Russian of Mikhaïl Lermontov

3. CLEAN PRIDE AND MUCKY PRIDE: PAROCHIALISM VERSUS PROVINCIALISM

Against the Cringe

The Irish poet Patrick Kavanagh made an important distinction between provincialism and parochialism. For him, provincialism was the mark of a locality which assumed that its own culture was inferior to that of the metropolis, to which it looked for direction: in Scotland we'd call that the Cringe. Parochialism, on the other hand, was a matter of unaffected celebration of local achievements. Yorkshire – as we'd expect – offers another source of good sense: in Charlotte Brontë's novel *Shirley*, there's a thoughtful working man, William Farren, who contrasts 'clean pride' with 'mucky pride'. The obverse of the cultural cringe is mucky pride – as in 'wha's like us?' Sure, parochialism can also become too inward-looking, but it resists pretension: it favours 'clean pride'. Despite recent significant advances, Fife's home-grown culture – and I stress home-grown - still suffers from provincialism: its cure is an outward-looking parochialism. In the local is the universal.

Back in 1995 the artist-impresario Richard Demarco delivered a guest lecture on Adam Smith at the Kirkcaldy campus of Fife College. He presented not the Smith who is used as an excuse for money-grubbing, but a mind and that mind's home-town, both of which looked to Europe – not cringingly, not seeking validation, but on terms of intellectual equality. The historian Christopher Harvie would later take up this theme in his essay, 'Reimagining Fife', in the first issue (2011) of the short-lived online periodical *The Pathhead*

Review, which I edited from Kirkcaldy (and, latterly, from an academic base in Connecticut). We'll return to those wider resonances of Adam Smith at a later point in the present book.

Regionalism and Patrick Geddes

Related to parochialism is regionalism, a concept which again has been articulated by an Irish poet – this time by John Hewitt, an Ulsterman. Coming from a part of the world racked by contending 'national' loyalties, Hewitt found in the 'region' a space with which both Protestant and Catholic, Republican and Unionist, could identify. Such a summary suggests both an over-simplification and an over-optimism that Hewitt would not have intended. As aspirations go, though, you could find a lot worse. In Scotland, regionalism was at the heart of the city-design (as opposed to town-planning) philosophy of Patrick Geddes, who in his book *City Development* (1904) drew up proposals for a revival of Dunfermline. These included an open-air auditorium, and folk museum exhibits on the Scandinavian model, together with educational spaces across the subject spectrum, in the context of a transformation of Pittencrieff Park and its environs – while fully respecting the existing contours of the town, contours historical, geographical and cultural. Geddes's ideas amounted to a people's-university-plus, one might say, fit for the former capital of a nation of north-western Europe.

4. A TESTAMENT OF FIFE – SECOND PART. MONIMAIL TO CRAIGTOUN

Monimail to Collessie:
We remember Marianna Lines,
Her studio at the foot of the slope,
To the plaque – in Scots – on the kirkyard wall:
Her work on the Picts, and her dying hope
For a better Scotland. She showed me all
The village's lore. She'd read the signs
Of her native America, in her year
Of exile, resuming its fury and fear.

Craigrothie, Ceres, to Pitscottie:
A family trip to Craigtoun Park,
Its Italian Garden in a wooded neuk,
Where, in the moonlight, sculpted stones
Leamed like stacks of brittle bones,
With gaping gods in their alcoves;
Nettles entwined in forgotten groves,
Terraces and balustrades collapsing into heaps
Of fungoid deliquescence that gave my mum the
        creeps,
As if grotto were the essence of grotty.
On the other hand, it suited me,
For my morbid teenage sensibility,
To delight in each drop-jawed ornamental spook,
Silent, ominous and stark.

5. 'BLEAK FERTILITY': ROBERT LOUIS STEVENSON AND FIFE

From his childhood home in Heriot Row, Edinburgh, Robert Louis Stevenson could see Fife. A more distant but also more panoramic view was available to him during his wanderings on the Pentland Hills, where in 1867 his family had taken the lease of Swanston Cottage. In his *Edinburgh: Picturesque Notes*, first published in book form in 1879, Stevenson stressed his native town's geographical and architectural uniqueness, by which the citizen and the visitor were presented with unusual and even unexpected prospects; there were, in fact, so many points at which one could make out the coast, the towns, the fields and the hills of the ancient 'Kingdom' on the other side of the Forth.

Stevenson's Scottish topography is by no means exclusively concerned with Edinburgh. It would be a mistake, therefore, to follow this literary vagabond through France, America and the south Pacific and ignore his explorations nearer – and just beyond - home. The capital both fascinated and restricted the romantic rebel in Stevenson; sooner or later he was bound to act on his curiosity regarding the rest of the nation - and to find useful material in the process. For example, long ago Nigel Tranter felt moved to remind readers (in *The Scots Magazine* of March 1968) that Stevenson was familiar with the coast of East Lothian and that this is reflected in many of his major and minor writings. The present article will consider the influence of the opposite shore. We should mention, however, that Stevenson's

Scotland also included the coast of Caithness, whose wild and rugged character he evoked in his essay 'The Education of an Engineer'; and it was at a cottage in Braemar, in 1881, that he conceived and wrote the first of his major works, *Treasure Island*. A reading of *Kidnapped,* which takes us round the coast of Scotland from east to west and through the Highlands, should convince anyone that Stevenson was more than just a smooth Edinburgh *littérateur* whose sights were set only in a southerly direction.

Stevenson's first connection with Fife was his nurse Alison Cunningham ('Cummy'), who was born in the coastal village of Torryburn, between Dunfermline and Culross. In 1885 Stevenson published *A Child's Garden of Verses*, which he dedicated to Alison, who had tended 'her laddie' during a childhood racked by chronic ill-health. However, her touch was not altogether soothing. She was a staunch Calvinist, and overwhelmed the young RLS with Old Testament stories, accounts of the Covenanters, all the horrors of Hell and martyrdom. Calvinism has had a curiously ambivalent influence on Scottish cultural psyche: on the one hand it has been narrow and repressive; on the other, it has stimulated imaginations eager for grim, passionate extremes. If there had been no 'Cummy', there might well have been no 'Thrawn Janet', 'Markheim', or Stevenson's most powerful tale of the diabolic, *The Strange Tale of Dr Jekyll and Mr Hyde.*

Those who want to know something of Alison's own point of view, perhaps to compare it with that of Stevenson, could turn to *Cummy's Diary*, edited by Robert T. Skinner and published in 1926.

Stevenson said of Fife: 'History broods over that part of the world like the easterly *haar.*' As far as he personally was concerned, a particularly striking instance of the history of the Covenanters here was their murder of Archbishop Sharpe on

Magus Muir, some kilometres south-west of St Andrews, in 1679. In the company of his father, Stevenson first visited the Muir in 1863, when he was getting on for thirteen. His ancestral cousin John Balfour of Kinloch, a Fife laird, had been one of the assassins, but that was not the most vivid aspect of the affair:

> The figure that always fixed my attention is that of Hackston of Rathillet, sitting in the saddle with his cloak about his mouth, and through all that long, bungling, vociferous hurly-burly, revolving privately a case of conscience. He would take no hand in the deed, because he had a private spite against the victim, and 'that action' must be sullied with no suggestion of a worldly motive; on the other hand, 'that action' in itself was highly justified, he had cast in his lot with 'the actors,' and he must stay there, inactive but publicly sharing the responsibility.

According to Jenni Calder in her 1980 biography of Stevenson, 'Hackston appealed not just because he was one of history's mysterious horsemen, but because of the twin forces of violence and conscience that were contained in him.' Again it is the Scots Calvinist tendency to juxtapose extremes, to dramatise human duality; it is, in fact, the all-pervasive characteristic of Stevenson's work. He made a childish attempt at a novel about Hackston of Rathillet, but abandoned it for lack of material.

The 1863 tour, recounted in the essay 'The Coast of Fife', was undertaken as a part of Stevenson senior's duties as a lighthouse engineer. Father and son made subsequent professional trips together. Indeed, it appeared that Louis would carry on the family tradition; he took classes in civil engineering at Edinburgh University. Inter-university rivalry may not be absent in the following comments, although he professes to be recalling here the 'crashing run of sea' on the coast:

> [...] I always imagine St Andrews to be an ineffectual seat of learning, and the sound of the east wind and the bursting surf to linger in its drowsy class-rooms and confound the utterance of the professor, until teacher and taught are alike drowned in oblivion, and only the sea-gull beats on the windows and the draught of the sea-air rustles in the pages of the open lecture.

He has the good grace, however, to refer the reader to the more expert judgment of his friend Andrew Lang. Lang, the well-known miscellaneous writer, was a St Andrews graduate and historian of the town.

Anstruther is the corner of Fife with which Stevenson was most acquainted, and it was here that engineering - his ostensible reason for being in the town - was losing out to his growing passion for literary activity. Fearing death at any moment, he scribbled late into the night. In a letter to his mother written in the summer of 1868, he made it clear that for him, art was above all else. He told her that he and a friend had gone to see a troupe of strolling players in Anstruther Town Hall. The performance was abysmal. Louis, however, observed to his friend that the company's manager 'had a soul above comic songs.' The friend retorted that the manager would be much happier as a common working man. Stevenson continued: 'I told him I thought he would be less happy earning a comfortable living as a shoemaker than he was starving as an actor, with such artistic work as he had to do. But the Phillistine [sic] wouldn't see it.' Respectable Mrs Stevenson read the words of a budding bohemian. Serious family conflict - another major Stevensonian theme - was looming large.

In the same letter Stevenson complained of 'this grey, grim, sea-beaten hole.' He was 'anxious to get back among trees and flowers and something less meaningless than this bleak fertility.' Bleak fertility: it was one of these phrases which, typically, brought opposites together (like 'black happiness' and 'judicious levity' elsewhere in his writings). In fact Stevenson found Anstruther to be rather more interesting than he cared to admit at this stage. After all, as he was aware, the town had already established itself on the literary map with the mock-heroic poem *Anster Fair* (1812) by one of its sons, William Tennant. In 'The Coast of Fife' Stevenson displays his fascination for the grotesque, the humorous-heroic (a very Scottish blend, that), and the romantic. His respective examples are the Shell House at the bridge between the two Anstruthers, Wester and Easter; the story of a clergyman's traumatic experience on the same bridge; and the appearance, at the manse of Anstruther Easter, of the Duke of Medina Sidonia, who had arrived in the harbour with his beleaguered portion of the great Armada. According to Dr Roger Swearingen, a leading Stevenson scholar, the young author had already made use of the second feature in a short story, 'The Curate of Anstruther's Bottle'. The manuscript has not been traced, but at least we have Stevenson's summary in 'The Coast of Fife'. As it is such an unfamiliar cameo of his narrative art, I present it here:

> Mr. Thomson, the 'curat' of Anstruther Easter, was a man highly obnoxious to the devout: in the first place, because he was a 'curat'; in the second place,

because he was a person of irregular and scandalous life; and in the third place, because he was generally suspected of dealings with the enemy of Man. These three disqualifications, in the popular literature of the time, go hand in hand; but the end of Mr. Thomson was a thing quite by itself, and in the proper phrase, a manifest judgment. He had been at a friend's house in Anstruther Wester, where (and elsewhere, I suspect), he had partaken of the bottle; indeed, to put the thing in our cold modern way, the reverend gentleman was on the brink of *delirium tremens*. It was a dark night, it seems; a little lassie came carrying a lantern to fetch the curate home; and away they went down the street of Anstruther Wester, the lantern swinging a bit in the child's hand, the barred lustre tossing up and down along the front of slumbering houses, and Mr. Thomson not altogether steady on his legs nor (to all appearance) easy in mind. The pair had reached the middle of the bridge when (as I conceive the scene) the poor tippler started in some baseless fear and looked behind him; the child, already shaken by the minister's strange behaviour, started also; in so doing, she would jerk the lantern; and for the space of a moment the lights and the shadows would be all confounded. Then it was that to the unhinged toper and the twittering child, a huge bulk of blackness seemed to sweep down, to pass them close by as they stood upon the bridge, and to vanish on the farther side in the general darkness of the night. 'Plainly the devil came for Mr. Thomson!' thought the child. What Mr. Thomson thought himself, we have no ground of knowledge; but he fell upon his knees in the midst of the bridge like a man praying. On the rest of the journey to the manse,

> history is silent; but when they came to the door, the poor caitiff, taking the lantern from the child, looked upon her with so lost a countenance that her little courage died within her, and she fled home screaming to her parents. Not a soul would venture out; all that night, the minister dwelt alone with his terrors in the manse; and when the day dawned, and men made bold to go about the streets, they found the devil had come indeed for Mr. Thomson.

Clearly Tam O'Shanter has his kindred 'spirits', in all senses of the word.

Stevenson's uncle, another John Balfour, was in the medical service in India and, as is mentioned in 'The Coast of Fife', was the last man to leave Delhi on the outbreak of the Mutiny. Dr Balfour consequently dedicated himself to fighting cholera at home, and crossed the Forth to deal with the epidemic in Leven. It was at Leven in 1871 that Louis met a workman with whom he launched into a discussion of education and politics. He was much impressed by the man's mind and compared him favourably with the clodhopping 'peasantry' of Suffolk. In his essay 'The Foreigner at Home' (1882) Stevenson remarks more generally on the intellectual and spiritual superiority of the Scots to the English. Perhaps Stevenson remembered the Leven labourer when he created Dand Elliott the shepherd-poet in his last and unfinished novel *Weir of Hermiston*.

However, there is another side to all this. 'Kailyard' writers such as 'Ian Maclaren' (Dr John Watson) tended to sentimentalise the 'lad o' pairts' from a humble background. Stevenson is not guilty of that, but his praise of the Scottish lower classes is implicitly challenged by another Scottish author, R.B. Cunninghame Graham, in his book of stories and sketches, *The Ipané* (1899). While agreeing that the Scot was better educated than the Englishman, Graham claimed that the former's schooling encouraged him to be brutish and competitive: 'In the social scale of human intercourse the bovine dweller in East Anglia is a prince compared to him.' Graham was no Anglified snob: he was in fact an ardent socialist and Scottish nationalist who refused to be complacent about the state of his own country.

1886 was an *annus mirabilis* for Stevenson. *The Strange Case of Dr Jekyll and Mr Hyde* and *Kidnapped* were published during this year; they are generally considered to be two of his greatest works. In the latter, David Balfour is forcibly put on board the brig *Covenant* of Dysart. Stevenson had a soft spot for Dysart, once an important international port in its own right, now a quiet corner of Kirkcaldy. In 'The Coast of Fife' Stevenson recalled 'the Dutch ships that lay in its harbour, painted like toys and with pots of flowers and cages of song birds in the cabin windows, and [...] one particular Dutch skipper who would sit all day in slippers on the break of the poop, smoking a long German pipe'. Dysart's extensive trade with the Dutch earned it the tag 'Little Holland'. Their present-day compatriots may pay holiday visits, but the foreign merchants have long gone. Dutch influence on the local architecture has been more enduring.

Stevenson was not the only late nineteenth-century novelist to make use of Dysart. John Buchan is arguably Stevenson's finest Scottish successor as a writer of adventure stories. He lived in nearby Pathhead during his boyhood, and in his early novel *A Lost Lady of Old Years* (1899), Dysart plays an important part in the action. Reference is made to the busy past of 'the little windworn town, where men's lips are always salt with the air from the sea, and a roaring east wind sweeps in the narrow lanes.' Stevenson would have been proud of him.

Nearing the completion of his momentous journey in *Kidnapped*, David Balfour, in company with Alan Breck, arrives at an inn in Limekilns, not far from 'Cummy's Torryburn. As a result of the persuasive powers of the two fugitives – including Alan's personal charm – the innkeeper's daughter promises to arrange their safe passage to the Lothian side. When night comes, David and Alan emerge from their hiding place as a boat approaches. To their astonishment, it is the girl herself. She counsels haste and silence, and proceeds to row them across the Forth. She sets them ashore near Carriden, shakes hands, then heads back for Limekilns before they can express their gratitude for such feminine gallantry.

That farewell to Fife is Stevenson at his romantic best. In the next year, 1867, shortly after the death of his father, Stevenson made his farewell to Scotland. From now on he was an exile. 'The Coast of Fife', as we have seen, draws on early memories; it was written in America. The posthumous collection *Songs of Travel* contains poems which were composed mostly in the south Pacific between 1888 and 1894, the year of Stevenson's death in Vailima, Samoa. One of the pieces is a blank verse tribute to his native land. Though 'Continents / And continental oceans intervene', he sees again the view from the Pentlands above Swanston. Edinburgh springs 'gallant from the shallows of her smoke, / Cragged, spired and turreted, her virgin fort, / Beflagged.' He looks further north.

> Last, the Forth
> Wheels ample waters set with sacred isles,
> And populous Fife smokes with a score of towns.

The land of 'bleak fertility' had retained its fascination, even in the tropics.

6. A TESTAMENT OF FIFE – THIRD PART. CUPAR TO LOWER LARGO

Cupar: Lebanon, Boudingait, Fluthers,
Cellardyke, the Anstruthers,

Where a quarryman's son of Aberdeen
Wrote his odyssey – from his back-green –

Alastair Mackie's rare word-store:
He brought Europe's poetry to our shore.

Pittenweem, St Monans, Isle of May,
Radiant panorama from Shell Bay.

Serpentine Walk to Lower Largo,
Polish soldiers with Scots quines, avoiding Uncle Joe.

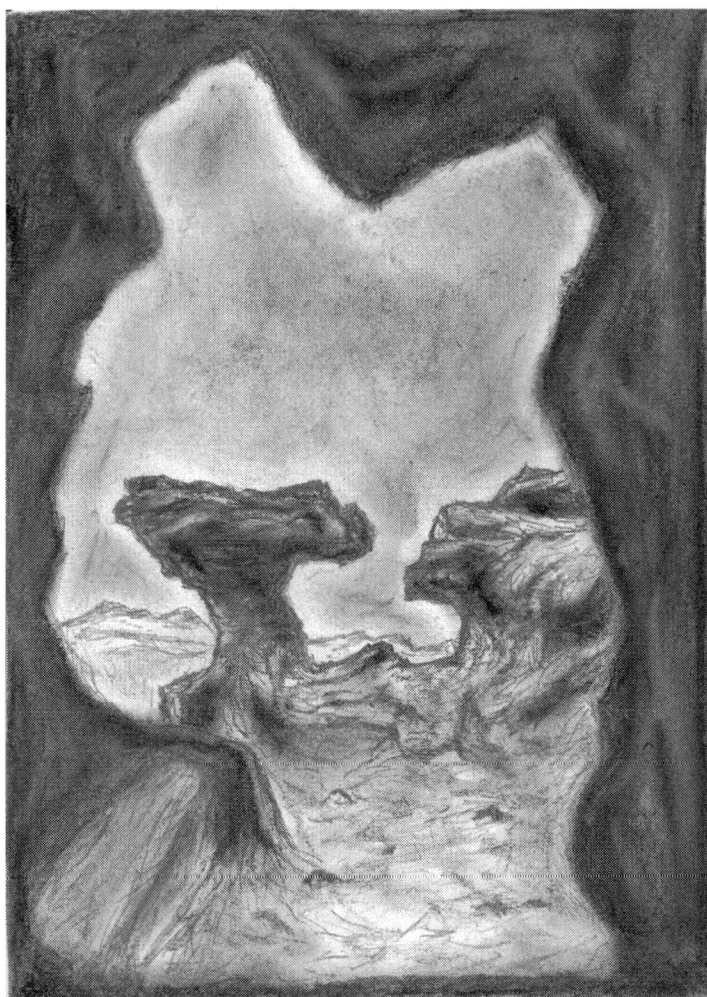

7. HERMAN MELVILLE, FIFE AND *MOBY-DICK*

Away O soul! hoist instantly the anchor!
Cut the hawsers—haul out—shake out every sail!

...

Sail forth— steer for the deep waters only,
Reckless O soul, exploring, I with thee, and thou with me,
For we are bound where mariner has not yet dared to go,
And we will risk the ship, ourselves and all.

WALT WHITMAN (1819-92) 'Passage to India'

1

The author of what is arguably *the* Great American Novel is one of Fife's unsung heroes. Is that a far-fetched remark, or at least bizarrely exaggerated? Possibly. However, Herman Melville (1819-91), whose best-known work is *Moby-Dick* (1851), was conscious of his Scottish ancestry, and specifically of his connections with Fife. He mentions the Kingdom a number of times in *Moby-Dick*, and there is a dramatic incident involving a Kirkcaldy clergyman in another Melville novel, *Israel Potter: His Fifty Years of Exile* (1855). Back in the 1980s, we used to take our bairns to Letham Glen, a beautiful park and woodland near Scoonie Kirk, where the American writer's direct ancestor, the Reverend Thomas Melville, was minister. From its present-day ruin, on a hill and surrounded by graves, you can see the Firth of Forth spread out before you: how apt for the minister's descendant, one of the great masters of maritime fiction.

During the 1980s, though, Letham Glen was for us a place for family recreation and that was it. Certainly around that time I was reviving my dormant interest in American literature but I had no idea then of the area's connection with Melville. I only discovered that later, quite unsystematically, while browsing in Hershel Parker's massive biography of Melville in an American university library. There I learned that in 1818 the writer's father Allan had visited Scotland, where he went about ancestry-hunting. On 26 May of that year, he paid a visit to the imposing Melville House, north of Ladybank, where he was received 'courteously enough' by his distant relation the Earl of Leven and Melville. It was far from a snooty cold-shouldering of a brash Yankee, but one suspects a certain bemusement on the part of the Scottish aristocrat. The earl's son, based in London, was less forthcoming, but Allan indomitably pursued his research and discovered that he was descended from the Melvilles of Carnbee, who in turn 'were related to Queen Margaret consort of Malcolm Canmere [sic] & came with her from Hungary' (Allan's words). Our contemporary, the Fife writer Christopher Rush (b. 1944), records that his great-grandfather met Herman Melville in 1890, and that the American's forebears are buried at Carnbee.

To return to the area around Scoonie, there is an early letter by Robert Louis Stevenson where he mentions a lane and a mill outside Leven. I suspect this may be the present-day Letham Glen, but I'm not sure. Stevenson claimed to be an admirer of Melville but I would doubt he'd be aware of any local connection. Moreover, and in spite of their common interest in the South Pacific, his comments on Melville are banal: he praised the American as a 'howling cheese', whatever that means, and objected pedantically to Melville's less than accurate transcriptions of Polynesian names. A far more serious response is that of the Scottish poet Hugh MacDiarmid (1892-1978), and we'll be returning to him.

Let us take a closer look at the Scottish (and Fife) references in Melville's books. In *Moby-Dick* he quotes whaling accounts from the east coast of Scotland; the sometimes callow narrator, Ishmael, tells us that porpoise meatballs were a delicacy much enjoyed by the monks of Dunfermline. You could read *Moby-Dick* simply for its compendium of facts about whaling! Melville has his tongue some way in his cheek when he lets Ishmael go on in this way. Curiously, it's all very pedantic but comically so.

A leading character in an earlier sea-faring book, *Omoo* (1847), Dr Long Ghost, is an uprooted Scot, at least as perceived by D.H. Lawrence in his sturdily unconventional essay on Melville; in the late and posthumously-published novella *Billy Budd*, the owner of the ship *The Rights-of-Man* is a radical, a reader of Tom Paine, from Dundee. In *Israel Potter*, cited at the beginning of this essay, the Scots-born American privateer John Paul Jones attempts to raid the coast of Fife, but a brave Kirkcaldy minister, the Reverend Robert Shirra, prays fervently on the beach for the invaders to be repulsed by a gale – which duly rages on the Firth of Forth. Jones and his crew are forced to retreat. The Dunfermline writer Daniel Thomson (1833-1908), in his own maritime novel *John Orrason* (1897), refers to 'the practical and prophetic Robert Shirra'. As regards Scotland's western shores, St Columba's Abbey at Iona features in Melville's long narrative poem *Clarel* from 1876.

2

Melville's work was little recognised in his own lifetime. Initial acclaim subsided when it became clear that he was attempting something bigger than a simple yarn of the sea. *Moby-Dick* was too big a book for nineteenth-century America to swallow. It's probably too big a book for an inward-looking, twenty-first century Britain to swallow: you can still take a degree in English without having read it.

Moby-Dick was first published in 1851. It wasn't a conventional, comforting piece of work. It's significant that Melville was at pains to point out that his friend Nathaniel Hawthorne (1804-64) was a darker and deeper writer than surface genialities would suggest. 'Certain it is', he wrote in 1850, 'that this great power of blackness in him [Hawthorne] derives its force from its appeals to that Calvinistic sense of Innate Depravity and Original Sin, from whose visitations, in some shape or other, no deeply thinking mind is always and wholly free.'

When Melville died in 1891, he was almost forgotten as a writer. Indeed the reaction to news of his death was one of surprise – people had assumed he'd already died long ago.

Moby-Dick is admittedly a baffling book. How might we read it? As a straightforward sea tale? An exciting story of the chase of a white whale? Many will read it on that level. Others won't. In our supposedly more ecologically-minded times, we might prefer to interpret the book as an indictment of the destruction of wildlife. We'd be going along with the ship's mate, Starbuck, when he challenges Captain Ahab: why take revenge on a poor dumb brute – it's a form of blasphemy. In another nineteenth-century American novel, James Fenimore Cooper's *The Pioneers* (1823) the leading character Natty Bumppo objects to the wanton destruction of the bird-shoot.

Widening out from this, we could read Melville's novel as a great hymn to Nature in all its grandeur; we might note the deeply spiritual identification of the First Nations of America with the land. In *Moby-Dick* we have the sea, the ocean, the archetypal symbol of eternity, of death, of depth. But more on this later.

Alternatively, we could read it as a novel about initiation. Our youngish narrator, Ishmael, tells us that he has *had* his hard knocks among the landlubbers, and that the sea naturally inclines him to mystical awareness – but because of Ahab and his obsession, towards which the voyage is directed, it becomes a literally overwhelming experience for him, i.e. it almost drowns Ishmael. He survives by a miracle, and is thus able to narrate the enormous book which we have in our hands. (It's a whale of a book ...) If Ishmael has learned anything from the experience, surely the 600 pages or so must testify to that. One lesson that he certainly masters is that someone from another race isn't necessarily going to remove your head and put the rest of you in the cooking pot – you may get friendly with him, you may depend on each other for survival.

Yet again this book may be an allegory about America. On the ship are hands of all races – whites, Indians, blacks, but also Polynesians, 'orientals' and so on. It's a microcosm of the 'melting pot' that America was reckoned to have become by the turn of the nineteenth century. America: secure in its sense of mission, in pursuit of a dream, an American dream, an American nightmare – and propelled by the certainties of a Puritan, Calvinist heritage. The book could be read as concerning an attempt to tame the wilderness – Ahab and his crew as pioneers: the watery wilderness would be acting as a metaphor for that of terra firma. Or instead of a single continent, here is that expanse – the *ocean* – which touches all continents; America could be acting like the ocean as it attempts to influence the rest of the world, and to aspire to become the world's only superpower.

Furthermore, taking up that point about Puritanism and Calvinism, isn't the novel a great moral and spiritual allegory of the soul – a nineteenth-century *Pilgrim's Progress*? Are opposites contrasted starkly in the Puritan-Calvinist black-and-white manner? Ahab, who looks like he's been cut from the stake, grim, *black*, against the *white* whale? (Here the racial overtones of black and white aren't relevant.) However, what about that streak of white that goes down Ahab's body – doesn't that suggest that it's all more complex than simple stark opposites?

That streak of white – Ishmael speculates that it may be a birthmark. In Melville's last novella, *Billy Budd*, the hero has a stutter, a handicap that seals his fate at a dramatic moment. One could call that the aural equivalent of a birthmark which is of course a visual phenomenon. Indeed, Melville explicitly refers, in *Billy Budd*, to Hawthorne's story, 'The Birthmark'.

Is the birthmark the flaw in all of us since the serpent tempted Eve – the mark of Cain?

In Calvinist theology, we can no more escape that mark than the scientist in Hawthorne's tale could succeed in removing the mark from his otherwise beautiful wife.

It's the mark of whatever has been *predestined* – and *predestination* is a very strong Calvinistic motif throughout *Moby Dick*. Ahab is in one sense a man of strong *will*, looking forward to Nietzsche's concept of the 'Superman' – the Übermensch – the Overman as it is more accurately translated. This strong will disdains lesser wills; Ahab sees the voyage as a titanic struggle, and not for the petty, worldly, commercial motives of the ship's owners.

Yet – a question of *will?* Ahab himself remarks on several occasions that *he's* predestined to undertake this mission. He's travelling on *rails*, according to an image he uses, a strange image for a journey by sea. He was predestined for this long, long before his birth – *God's* will is as timeless as the rolling of the waves that rolled before our birth and will continue to roll after our death.

3

In 1830 Melville's father, Allan, went bankrupt; that was not an ideal condition in thrusting, striving America. Young Herman worked variously as a bank clerk, salesman, farmworker, schoolteacher. He attempted a course in engineering and surveying. He began to write.

In 1839 he signed on as a cabin boy, and was initiated into the horrors of life at sea. On a Pacific voyage he jumped ship; later in his maritime career he was involved in a mutiny. During a spell in Hawaii, he worked in a bowling-alley. In due course, however, there appeared a series of books based on his experiences – *Typee* (1846) – 'Typee' is the name of a Polynesian island tribe, followed in the next year by *Omoo*; 'Omoo' is a Polynesian word meaning a 'rover'. Indeed *Moby-Dick* could be taken as a book about the archetypal rover, the wanderer: Ishmael has the lone rebel's need to cut loose from the land, Ahab is the accursed wanderer in the line of the Wandering Jew or the Flying Dutchman (the latter of whom is the subject of an 1887 painting by the American artist Albert Pinkham Ryder [1847-1917].)

It was in *Typee* that we encounter the first instance of

what Melville would call the 'isolato', in this sketch of the narrator's friend Toby: 'He was one of that class of rovers you sometimes meet at sea, who never reveal their origin, never allude to home, and go rambling over the world as if pursued by some mysterious fate they cannot possibly elude.' In *John Orrason,* Daniel Thomson has a character who is a Scottish version of this archetype, with obvious variations: 'the merchant planter of Falmouth [Antigua] was a Scotchman – one of that numerous, and nearly ubiquitous, clan called the "Scots abroad", who had an intense love for the old home but found fortune smiled more blandly and more continuously in lands beyond the seas.' It's Thomson's main (and eponymous) character, however, who is more of the troubled 'isolato': 'Shall I, the wanderer, have the dreary task of speaking my identity into the ears of those who would rather shun my presence, who would find no comeliness therein nor music to my voice? These, the ancient enemies of his peace, *would* come back to him, and whisper eternally their suggestions in his heart.'

Typee posits a Garden of Eden, a tribe living communally, free and easy in their sexual behaviour, lying about all day in the sun while 'civilised' America locks itself into overdrive in the dark cities. There was something in Melville which favoured uncomplicated nature against what he called 'Cain's city and citified man' in *Billy Budd.* One of Melville's most haunting short stories is 'Bartleby the Scrivener' (1853), which is doubtless based on his own experiences of clerking in New York. Bartleby the scrivener or clerk wastes away in the gloomy, routine-based environment of lawyers' offices; a brick wall is only three feet from the window by his desk.

Bartleby makes a bleakly anti-heroic refusal of this: when his boss asks him to undertake a particular task, he replies 'I would prefer not to.' That's his refrain – 'I would prefer not to'. His boss, the narrator, feels unable to sack him and tries in vain to help him. After Bartleby's death, the boss learns that the clerk once worked in the Dead-Letter Office in Washington – that is, he had to go through items of human communication that never reached their addressees.

This story is more than one about an uncommonly soft boss and his recalcitrant employee – it evokes the apparent meaninglessness, the spiritual and human emptiness of the modern city. It's a story that seems ahead of its time, that might belong more to the twentieth century and the urban labyrinths of Franz Kafka – though it does have its nineteenth-century analogues, in this respect, with the poetry of Baudelaire and the darker novels of Dickens and Dostoevsky.

Even so, the South Sea islanders, the Typee, are not really an alternative. Melville is still very much the Euro-American more at home, for all that, in New York City. As for the Garden of Eden symbolism, the serpent of Genesis has his equivalent in this seeming South Seas Paradise; Melville's narrator may have found his new Eve in the form of the 'beauteous Fayaway' – but there is cannibalism. Much later in the century there would be a different meeting of the Presbyterian and the Polynesian, when Robert Louis Stevenson made his final home in Samoa.

Other books based on Melville's wanderings are *Mardi* (1849), *Redburn* (also 1849) and *White-Jacket* (1850). *Redburn* is a European book, or at least an 'English' book, based on his experiences in Liverpool and London. In 1857 came the bizarre novel *The Confidence Man*, on which more shortly.

As its subtitle 'The Ambiguities' would suggest, *Pierre* (1852) is a complex psychological novel, again, more appreciable in post-Freudian times than in the mid-nineteenth century. It anticipates Stevenson's *The Strange Case of Dr Jekyll and Mr Hyde* (1886), even as that book itself anticipates Freud. Pierre Glendinning is a ponderously idealistic young man who has grown up in a sheltered, upper-class Upstate New York environment. He's an effete mummy's boy whose sudden sexual awakening – which will prove to be incestuous – leads to a state of split personality:

> He entered the hall unnoticed, passed up to his chamber, and hurriedly locking the door in the dark, lit his lamp. As the summoned flame illuminated the room, Pierre, standing before the round center-table, where the lamp was placed, with his hand yet on the brass circle which regulated the wick, started at a figure in the opposite mirror. It bore the outline of Pierre, but now strangely filled with features transformed, and unfamiliar to him; feverish eagerness, fear, and nameless forebodings of ill! [...] Pierre now seemed distinctly to feel two antagonistic agencies within him; one of which was just struggling into his consciousness, and each of which was striving for the mastery; and between whose respective final ascendencies, he thought he could perceive, though but shadowly, that he himself was to be the only umpire.

Forty-five years later, in 1897, Melville's compatriot Mark Twain would write a short and pithy analysis of *Jekyll and Hyde.*

Beyond the deceptively decorous milieu of Pierre's township of Saddle Meadows, there are deep woods with strange rock formations, including an outcrop which the young man calls the Terror Stone; he speculates that if one could crawl under it, one would be crushed to death if its 'mute massiveness' should collapse. This appeals to his more suicidal moods. 'Pierre', it's more than hinted, is French for 'stone'. A few pages on, the patterns of symbolism, of this novel and of *Moby-Dick*, seem to coalesce in this passage:

> Still wandering through the forest, his eye pursuing its ever-shifting shadowy vistas; remote from all visible haunts and traces of that strangely wilful race, who, in the sordid traffickings of clay and mud, are ever seeking to denationalize the natural heavenliness of their souls; there came into the mind of Pierre, thoughts and fancies never imbibed within the gates of towns; but only given forth by the atmosphere of primeval forests, which, with the eternal ocean, are the only unchanged general objects remaining to this day, from those that originally met the gaze of Adam. For so it is, that the apparently most inflammable or evaporable of all earthly things, wood and water, are, in this view, immensely the most endurable.

Weirdly-shaped outcrops of rock in forests were often sites of worship, by America's First Nations, of the Great Spirit. Their equivalents in Scotland are similarly mysterious and tend to accumulate dark legends: a dramatic example of this is the Bonnet or Bannet Stane, just within the county boundary of Fife, on the slope of West Lomond. Of this cluster of outcrops, the late Marianna Lines has written, in her book *The Traveller's Guide to Sacred Scotland* (2014): 'The soft rock has been hollowed out below the Bonnet Stane by people long ago into a cave where a hermit once lived. Known as the Maiden's Bower, the story goes that long ago a young maiden fell in love with the son of a rival family and the stone was their meeting place. One day she saw her father's men ambush and kill her lover. She then refused to return home, spending the rest of her life in the cave and becoming known locally as a saint.'

Melville's *Pierre* possesses much of that lurid, ballad-like quality.

4

In *Moby Dick*, Ahab tells Starbuck, the ship's mate, that 'all visible objects are but pasteboard masks', but that some unknown yet reasoning thing is there behind the unreasoning mask. 'If man will strike, strike through the mask!' Thus Ahab aims to strike through the whale, which to him is something more than what it physically seems.

We have to dive below the surface of things – Melville says he loves those who *dive* – in order to get to the deeper, darker realities. The ocean is a symbol for the hidden, the unconscious, the deeps of human psychology, or – in religious terms – the soul.

The Scottish poet Hugh MacDiarmid draws strongly on Melville and *Moby Dick* in his long poem *A Drunk Man Looks at the Thistle* (1926). The thistle, with its hidden roots, is a symbol of the psyche – both Scottish and universal – and that plant undergoes many transformations in the course of the poem. MacDiarmid's drunk man recognises Melville as a Scot with a Scottish seriousness about metaphysics, as a fellow intellectual wanderer; the drunk man and Melville could be said to be restless Faustian questers and questioners. So: the roots of the thistle can modulate into the body of the whale, of Leviathan. We can't be content with what's above the ground, or with what's above the surface of the ocean.

It isn't coincidental that MacDiarmid's uncommonly perceptive drunk man is equally engaged with Dostoevsky. The American and the Russian are often associated as two writers who take the novel into a dimension beyond what is normally expected of that literary form. In his book *Aspects of the Novel* (1927), E.M. Forster devotes a chapter to 'Prophecy', in which Dostoevsky and Melville loom large. A few pages on from his discussion of Dostoevsky's *Brothers Karamazov*, he remarks of Melville's masterpiece: 'The essential in *Moby Dick*, its prophetic song, flows athwart the action and the surface morality like an undercurrent.' Henry James's words on *The House of the Seven Gables* (1851) by Melville's colleague Nathaniel Hawthorne, could be applied even more strongly to *Moby-Dick*: 'A large and generous production, pervaded with that vague hum, that indefinable echo, of the whole multitudinous life of man, which is the real sign of a great work of fiction.' Lewis Mumford maintains that '"Moby-Dick" is a labyrinth, and that labyrinth is the universe.'

Captain Ahab's phrase 'pasteboard masks' is especially resonant. Our writer's late novel, *The Confidence Man* of 1857, is subtitled 'His Masquerade'. We might think back to another American writer immediately preceding Melville in his career, Edgar Allan Poe, and the masquerades which take place in his stories, notably in 'The Cask of Amontillado', where the masks are removed and horrors are thus revealed. In *The Confidence Man*, the title-character assumes various disguises and tricks his fellow-passengers on a Mississippi steamboat. Here is a white man's version of the 'trickster' archetype which we encounter in Native American and African-American folklore: think of Br'er Rabbit who belongs to both First Nation and African-American legends. In his book, however, Melville is satirising the gullibility, the materialism and the shallowness of mid-century America. (The shallow public, one might think, who neglected Melville for less honest entertainers ...)

Here was yet another oddball book which has had more of a following in our more cynical times.

Yet the main character of *The Confidence Man*, together with the Mississippi setting, look forward to Mark Twain's *Huckleberry Finn* (1884) and the two con-men who take refuge in Huck's and Jim's raft. It's the 'innocent' Huck who can see through these chancers – the one who claims to be the Duke of Bridgewater (or Bilgewater as his pal calls him); the other who says he's the exiled 'Dolphin', i.e. Dauphin of France, King Louis XVII.

The Duke and the King can fool the public for a good while – until they're rumbled and chased out of town, duly tarred and feathered. In both Melville and Twain there's much humour but it usually has dark undertones. Alas, since I lectured on Melville at various Scottish and American universities, a one-liner of George Carlin's has gained new traction: 'In America, *anyone can become president.* That's the problem.' Replace 'anyone' with 'a con-man' and there you have it.

Billy Budd was completed on 19 April 1891: that's the date written on the manuscript. Melville died in September of that year. However, the story wasn't published until 1924 when the climate was more favourable. Billy Budd is the 'Handsome Sailor' much loved by the crew and by the Captain. Some have suggested that Captain Vere is the secret father of Budd, who has said that he was a foundling, having been asked that perennial American question, 'Where do you come from? How were you born?' (The setting is English, but *Billy Budd* is still a subtly American book.)

Billy has the beauty and innocence of Adam, innocence which *may* be attractive, *is* certainly not adequate in the face of the corrupt world. A ship's officer, Claggart, conceives a strange, demonic hatred of Billy, and challenges him in the presence of Captain Vere. Billy's stutter prevents him replying and he lashes out with his fist. The blow kills Claggart.

Claggart's hate could be interpreted as almost a twisted love, a variant on the homosexuality that's often not very much below the surface in Melville's work. Claggart is described in images of sophisticated, intellectual evil – of the snake in Eden. (The Hawthornean notion of America as an Eden not immune from corruption is also, as we've seen, a Melvillean notion.)

Captain Vere resists the promptings of 'Nature', which would compassionately pardon this boy who's been provoked. Struggling against his humane feelings, Vere must conform to the dictates of society, of law, of his duty to the King – his responsibility to a sinful, post-Fall, 'civilisation'. According to naval law, Billy must hang from the yard-arm for striking and killing a superior officer.

The story calls on the reader's sympathy for Captain Vere as much as for the young man (that possible son of his) whom he condemns. Vere is very much a loner in relation to his fellow-officers; he's an aristocrat, bookish, reflective – another one of Melville's 'isolatoes'. The Captain is given the epithet 'starry Vere'.

Moby-Dick dwells much on how the ocean draws out a philosophical, as well as a poetic, reflectiveness. It encourages a spiritual awakening – and 'awakening' is a key word in understanding nineteenth-century American literature. We obtain a foretaste of this spirituality in the sermon of Father Mapple in his pulpit made from a boat, and in the comically earnest banter of those good Quakers, Captains Peleg and

Bildad. In Bildad we see the North American blend of piety and commercialism, of God and Mammon; he exhorts the men not to go whaling on the Lord's Day, but also not to miss a chance of profit should a whale appear – such would be to neglect God's gifts! (He also makes a point of telling one of the men to avoid fornication.)

This spiritual grotesquerie, played out on the shore, serves to highlight, by contrast, the more expansive, resonant spirituality of the ocean. The *Pequod*'s voyage could stand for any voyage, including those of the Mississippi novels of Melville and Twain – the voyage is that of the human soul in its passage through life. 'Passage to more than India!' is a line from the poem by Walt Whitman which provides the epigraph for the present essay. On that voyage, the individual human soul is divided – Ahab is divided against himself; Starbuck warns him: 'Let Ahab beware of Ahab! Beware of thyself, old man.'

The crew talk of Ahab having made a pact with the devil. Ahab indeed 'baptises' a harpoon 'in the name of the devil'. The devil might be *inside* Ahab. This certainly inhabits the same spiritual territory as Goethe's *Faust* or Stevenson's *Dr Jekyll and Mr Hyde*. Ahab has his alter ego in the Parsee Fedallah: here there is much talk of the one inhabiting the other's shadow. A Jungian interpretation would make much of this.

Ahab is a Faustian alchemist, blending the elements fire, water and air. Not earth, however: he left that behind at Nantucket. He doesn't *make* gold – the gold's already there (in an incentivising doubloon offered to the crew), and he is not sailing for money, unlike the ship's owners. Gold is of the element earth.

As for the whale, it could be the embodiment of everything in life which frustrates us, everything that seems malevolently ranged against us, blocking our way. In Ibsen's play *Peer Gynt*, the hero is up against something not dissimilar in the form of a great mythical blob called the Great Bøyg – but Peer, being an archetypal chancer, goes *round* rather than *through* the Great Bøyg. Ahab is made of sterner stuff and is determined to go *through* the Great Whale – with his harpoon rather than his person, that is. The Scottish poet Tom Scott (1918-95) wrote a verse sequel in which Ahab survives, reaches the shore of an island, and is worshipped by the natives as a God.

Ahab's a loner, an 'isolato'; so is Ishmael, at both the beginning and the end of the novel. Ahab, though, resents having to *rely* on other people – especially on the 'blockhead carpenter' who supplies his artificial leg. 'Cursed be that mortal inter-indebtedness', he growls; but we can't escape the necessity of 'inter-indebtedness' – the extreme individualism of America denies the reality of our condition as social beings.

Solidarity – as Joseph Conrad recognised in his own maritime fiction – is a necessity as much aboard a ship as on land: even more so aboard a ship. The South Sea islander Queequeg teaches Ishmael the lesson of interdependence. It seems that this solidarity, even love, is the one thing that redeems us from the indifferent or even malevolent immensity. This relates very much to the novel's Whitman-like hymn to democracy, to the common working man; we would catch here an echo of Burns's 'the rank is but the guinea's stamp':

> Men may seem detestable as joint stock-companies and nations; knaves, fools, and murderers there may be; men may have mean and meagre faces; but man, in the ideal, is so noble and so sparkling, such a grand and glowing creature, that over any ignominious

blemish in him all his fellows should run to throw their costliest robes. That immaculate manliness we feel within ourselves, so far within us, that it remains intact though all the outer character seem gone; bleeds with keenest anguish at the undraped spectacle of a valor-ruined man. Nor can piety itself, at such a shameful sight, completely stifle her upbraidings against the permitting stars. But this august dignity I treat of, is not the dignity of kings and robes, but that abounding dignity which has no robed investiture. Thou shalt see it shining in the arm that wields a pick or drives a spike; that democratic dignity which, on all hands, radiates without end from God; Himself! The great God absolute! The centre and circumference of all democracy! His omnipresence, our divine equality!

If, then, to meanest mariners, and renegades and castaways, I shall hereafter ascribe high qualities, though dark; weave round them tragic graces; if even the most mournful, perchance the most abased, among them all, shall at times lift himself to the exalted mounts; if I shall touch that workman's arm with some ethereal light; if I shall spread a rainbow over his disastrous set of sun; then against all mortal critics bear me out in it, thou Just Spirit of Equality, which hast spread one royal mantle of humanity over all my kind! Bear me out in it, thou great democratic God!

It has to be said that, owing to a dour conservatism, Joseph Conrad's notion of solidarity does not extend to working folk and their political struggles. The Nigerian writer Chinua Achebe attacked the racism inherent in *Heart of Darkness*. Nevertheless, Melville as a fellow-sailor would have nodded assent to the conclusion of Conrad's unfortunately-titled novel *The Nigger of the 'Narcissus'* (1897): 'Haven't we, together and upon the immortal sea, wrung out a meaning from our sinful lives? Good-bye brothers! You were a good crowd. As good a crowd as ever fisted with wild cries the beating canvas of a heavy foresail; or tossing aloft, invisible in the night, gave back yell for yell to a westerly gale.'

Solidarity, or love, thus redeems us from ourselves. To be an 'Overman' like Ahab, or a loner, is not enough. We discern the limitations of being an 'isolato', whether that be Ahab, Ishmael, Pierre, Bartleby, or any other example in Melville's writings. Melville himself may have enjoyed his solitude but suffered from his loneliness – not least that caused by the indifference of the reading public. Even Ahab, we learn, has pangs for the family which he has left behind.

Finally, although *Moby Dick* is a deeply serious book, it's by no means a solemn one. It could serve as an illustration of the saying 'Humour is the blossom on the tree of profundity'. Stubb is an important character here. He gives us the foil to the eternal verities as so grimly uttered by Ahab. He's the scherzo in this great symphony of a book. His humour *is* serious – it grows out of extreme and desperate situations – but how else would you react? You have to relieve the tension. So Stubb as it were spiritually 'captures' the whale, and also even God, by calling them 'jokers'; he cuts the waves, too, down to size in his wee song – 'Such a funny, sporty, gamy, jesty, joky, hoky-poky lad is the Ocean, oh!'

Let Edgar Allan Poe have the last word: 'And *laugh* – but *smile* no more'.

8. A TESTAMENT OF FIFE – FOURTH PART. METHIL TO THE CAVES AND ABANDONED PITS

In halls of Methil and Buckhaven
Speakers in their twenties and thirties,
Women and men, call for action on these times:
Jobs have gone, libraries have closed,
Bairns lack teachers and hospitals, doctors.
Nurses struggle while Lord High Numpties
Scribble against 'élites', for six-figure fees.
Westminster overtakes any G and S farce,
And the Butcher's Apron is too soiled to wipe your
        arse.

The silence of caves and pits:
Tenebrous legends and vexed histories,
Down the part-threaded labyrinths of the centuries.

Children bleed in the desert
Courtesy of UK OK;
Princes and salesmen embrace
In well-laundered array.
The Tories expect your thanks
'That at least you have foodbanks,
And for the soporific condition
Of Her Majesty's Opposition –

Who are good chaps, really, craving trinkets from the
        queen:
They'll all vote for a Trident submarine!
So: laugh with the Etonian, admire his male erectness,
And let's hear no more of your whingeing Scotch
        correctness!'

9. WALKIN IN FIFE: DUNCAN GLEN, MARKINCH AND POINTS NORTH

Walkin in Fife, a poem-sequence by Duncan Glen (1933-2008), is mainly about *walkin OOT* in Fife. The sequence charts the poet's courtship through one of Scotland's most serenely beautiful (and untouristed) landscapes — the area to the south-east of the Lomond Hills, the county's highest points. This was the scene of my own courtship: for a while my future wife, Leslie-raised, lived in Cadham and we used to enjoy both weekend strolls through Balbirnie Park and more ambitious hikes up the Lomond slopes. I and Duncan Glen – with whom I worked on many literary projects - were aware that though holidaymakers tend not to byde there, the area has attracted writers. Alan Bold (1943-1998) – like Duncan, an all-round man of letters - referred to Balbirnie memorably as a 'Dantesque wood'; he inhabited a cottage there for most of the latter half of his life. The historian Trevor Royle and the actor John Bett were his neighbours for a while, as was an American-in-residence, Bill Costley, whom Bold welcomed in the most civilised way imaginable — by anthologising his poetry.

I love the way *Walkin in Fife* follows Glen's progress with his lady up to that final shortest walk of all the walks — to face the Rev. Davidson of St Drostan's Kirk, Markinch. The course of true love doesn't always run smoothly, but in this story at least it does so gently. The tender comedy radiates through the landscape and is in turn radiated by it. For much (but not all) of the sequence, we're talking of the south-west / north-east curve of Markinch Station, St Drostan's, Cuinin Hill, Star village, and

Carriston. The poet's efforts to impress the belle are invariably inept, as she makes laconically clear, but his self-knowledge and consequent self-mockery are compensatingly endearing. Come to think of it, it was the same in my case, as my wife would probably not attest.

The first poem invokes the native wildlife such as Balbirnie's hoolets (owls) and squirrels, but I find myself thinking also of peacocks. Why? They, along with descendants of the king's squirrels, were a feature of Dunfermline's Pittencrieff Glen (of which more later in the present book), but I don't recall any at Balbirnie. Yet there's a Fife thing going on here. The poet wants to involve the sight of hoolets and squirrels, as well as of stars, in the courtship. Freudians might talk of a certain projection, a cathexis, of the lover's psychic energy, even as he loves, upon external phenomena. More simply, it might be a case of trying to be one with nature, of signalling that courtship itself belongs crucially to the cycle of nature. It was Dunfermline's, Fife's, and Scotland's greatest poet — Robert Henrysoun — who reinforced the Aesopian tradition of using animal behaviour as extended metaphor for the all-too-human; not sentimental anthropomorphising, but yielding insights which are wise because they are funny and funny because they are wise.

The peacock is the poet with his just pride, but who occasionally gets a bit above himself; the squirrel is also the poet, but, prompted by his lady, is capable of taking himself healthily down again. Fife is a microcosm of Scotland in its noble uplands (Lomonds), palaces (Falkland, celebrated in a poem in Glen's sequence), its proud face in the direction of its sometime Danish invader. That's the peacock. Fife is also the dour banter of its working folk, quick to put down any 'Edinburry' pretensions, our local version, if you like, of what is called (with unfitting grandiosity) the 'reductive idiom'. Enter the squirrel. And what a cheeky fella he is. The peacock can he pompous, overblown; and yet the squirrel can often be the spirit who denies, gratuitously destructive of endeavours that attempt sincerely to be enhancing (ho-hum), which try to challenge and expand our consciousness. Sure, we need both beauties at their best, setting off each other in a creative dialectic; a poor Faust it would be without his Mephistopheles, and vice versa. In this sequence, the 'squirrel' incursions aren't always generated by the poet and his lady; they can be external presences, suddenly irrupting and vaguely threatening, such as the a.w.o.l. inmate from the Springfield asylum ('Encounter') and the tinkers up Cuinin Hill ('The Unkent'). What a nightmarish image that is of the 'daurk bulbous tents', with the couple walking 'very quaitly close thegither but fast / at the soond o their howlin and wailin that's mebbe / singin.' The 'peacock'-y aspects of courtship are given short shrift here, but then a little reality doesn't detract from the romance — far from it: it gives it an edge and a flavour. The couple can still proceed laughingly to Star village and to that splendid panorama which greets you when you descend Cuinin on the Star side. (Nothing prepares you for it when you ascend from the Markinch side, from that more hemmed-in, tree-and-dyke-lined approach.)

A love affair acquires an extra dimension when there's an awareness of its taking place within the larger narratives of history. Lovers do not necessarily have to go out of their way to direct cathectic energy onto this, i.e. they don't have to be conscious of it. In literature, though, that consciousness has to be there, subtly or otherwise. Antony and Cleopatra play out their drama against the clash of their respective realms; Chekhov's lady-with-the-dog and her lover contemplate a Black Sea that rolled before they were born and will roll after their deaths. *Walkin in Fife* presents the couple in Falkland, where the poet expounds his literary as much as his historical knowledge to his sceptical partner, referring to the Duke of Rothesay's dungeon death in Scott's *The Fair Maid of Perth*. At St Monans he detains her with tales of sixteenth-century Dutch settlers in Buckhaven: 'You didnae speak to me aw the wey hame.' Duncan Glen-as-himself — to distinguish him from his persona in these poems — went on to fare much better as a local historian: witness, especially, his book on Kirkcaldy.

So, finally, what is the sequence's 'Black Sea' moment? It would have to be the poem 'Winter Peak', with that intense perception of East Lomond as 'a real Matterhorn set down in pastoral Fife.' It transcends both peacock and squirrel modes, and acts as counterpoint to the grotesqueries of the 'Encounter' past and 'The Unkent' to come. It causes the lady to break through her reserve, to hold the poet close, and thus makes possible the 'happy run thegither' and that quietly victorious stance before the Reverend Davidson.

10. A TESTAMENT OF FIFE – FIFTH PART. RAVENSCRAIG TO KIRKCALDY

RAVENSCRAIG ELEGY
For Duncan Glen

Cave and turret: silence with presence,
And an eldritch echo across the Forth.
Ten years since we walked to lunch at the Man in the
      Rock,
Discoursing of books and pamphlets: daftness and
      laughter.
There were labours past and to come,
Above Dysart harbour, which welcomes its children
      home.

Nature unknowingly saves for us her artefacts:
The stone seat by the path, the twisted tree where a
      girl plays with her dog,
So from the flux and flummox you rescued song.
The gull's cry and the wave's lap unmake to re-make
      themselves, as your long
Stravaiging halts, resumes and re-enacts.

TOM HUBBARD

IN A KIRKCALDY WARKIN-CLESS AIRT

Nine thoosan days hae deed sin you bade here;
A hunner raiths, frae cranreuch throu ti sun;
As mony dunts, thir five-an-twenty year,
Upon your hert, seem aa that you hae won.
An yit the schuil, the store, the clertie grun
Your bairnspiel kent, byde on. Hit's juist the fowk
Are new: their leid comes fremmit ti your tongue,
You buik-leired doctor goavin like a gowk.
Why come ye back? Whit notion gars ye snowk
At whit's nae mair yer ain? Are ye sae fasht
Bi a tuimness at yer hichts, that ye wad howk
This roch an routhie syle? Your life's but tasht.
You tak your leave fir aye, as gin you'd thocht
o aa you'd tint, but cuid recover nocht.

11. ADAM SMITH'S
'SYMPATHY' SYMPHONY

At the beginning of an essay on 'Nietzsche and the Germans', the historian A.J.P. Taylor remarked that 'Every great movement crucifies its founder'. Some readers may recall a 1975 cartoon by the inimitable 'Trog' (Wally Fawkes) showing a couple of KGB goons hauling off Karl Marx for leafleting in the heart of the Soviet capital.

A slither of dubious disciples has continued to attend Adam Smith. His name is taken in vain by market fundamentalists who derive their apologetics for 'trickle-down' economics from Smith's image of the providential 'unseen hand' which was to guide us, or at least some of us, in the end, to the promised land.

Smith himself could not have foreseen — and cannot be blamed — for the dire eventualities of laissez-faire. These manifested themselves, however, soon enough in William Blake's 'dark satanic mills' of the Industrial Revolution, and instructions to the 'undeserving poor', like Jo the destitute and sick street-sweeper in Dickens's *Bleak House*, to 'move on'. Just up the brae from Adam Smith's Kirkcaldy birthplace, in Kirk Wynd, there lodged the thunderous Thomas Carlyle who deplored that 'cash payment' had become 'the sole nexus of man to man' (*Chartism*, chapter 6). He warned that by long hours of tending to machines, human beings had themselves become 'mechanical in head and heart'. Such, it seemed, was the ultimate outcome of Adam Smith's 'division of labour'. John Ruskin, the half-Scottish seconder to Carlyle, insisted that 'it is not, truly speaking, the labour that is divided; but the men: – Divided into mere segments of men – broken into small fragments and crumbs of life; so that all the little piece of intelligence that is left in a man is not enough to make a pin, or a nail, but exhausts itself in making the point of a pin or the head of a nail.' (*The Stones of Venice*, vol. 2, chapter 6). Clearly, readers of *The Wealth of Nations* would recognise an ironic echo of Smith in Ruskin's utterance.

Thatcherite dogmatists who extol the supposed virtues of universal selfishness and inequality are less inclined to invoke much (if not most) of the rest of Adam Smith's œuvre, and indeed would be embarrassed by Smith's strictures, in *The Wealth of Nations*, on the conspiratorial nature of merchants' foregatherings. In *The Theory of Moral Sentiments* (1759), Smith writes a praise-poem-in-prose to human 'sympathy', a value little-prized by the far-right of the twenty-first century: 'How selfish soever man may be supposed, there are evidently some principles in his nature, which interest him in the fortune of others, and render their happiness necessary to him, though he derives nothing from it except the pleasure of seeing it.'

The sheer variety of Adam Smith's intellectual interests, and the elegant wit and humanity with which they are infused, is not generally celebrated. During September 2017, I was involved in events to mark the centenary of Russian studies at Glasgow University, and as I approached the grand staircase of that neo-Gothic pile on Gilmorehill, heading for a conference session, I became intrigued by the larger-than-life statue of one of the university's best-known professors, Adam Smith. He stood with his right arm outstretched, looking for all the world as if he were conducting an orchestra. Would Mozart have looked like this, I wondered, if he'd lived into late middle age? Some months after this, I was reading Smith's essay 'Of the Nature of that Imitation which takes place in what are called The Imitative Arts' and was struck by this passage: 'A well-composed concerto of instrumental Music, by the number and variety of the instruments, by the variety of the parts which are performed by them, and the perfect concord or correspondence of all these different parts; by the exact harmony or coincidence of all the different sounds which are heard at the same time, and by that happy variety of measure which regulates the succession of those which are heard at different times, presents an object so agreeable, so great, so various, - and so interesting, that alone, and without suggesting any other object, either by imitation or otherwise, it can occupy, and as it were fill up, completely the whole capacity of the mind, so as to leave no part of its attention vacant for thinking of anything else. In the contemplation of that immense variety of agreeable and melodious sounds, arranged and digested, both in their coincidence and in their succession, into so complete and regular a system, the mind in reality enjoys not only a very great sensual, but a very high intellectual, pleasure, not unlike that which it derives from the contemplation of a great system in any other science.'

That's it, I thought: our delight in a piece by Smith's contemporaries such as Haydn or Mozart, our attention being wholly engaged, is akin to our delight in grasping Aristotle, Marx, Freud, or for that matter Adam Smith or any other brilliantly labyrinthine thinker: we respond to the ingenuity of structure. As a young student in my Senior Honours year at Aberdeen University, I strove to get my head round – or rather into – Coleridge's *Biographia Literaria*. Around that time I had been introduced to Havergal Brian's Violin Concerto, and I felt, naïvely enough, an affinity between those two works which were otherwise so surely disparate. It was if I was wondering: how did Coleridge and Brian, in each masterpiece, arrive at *there* from *here*? Over forty years later I found, in my fellow-townsman Adam Smith, an explanation for my seemingly bizarre juxtapositioning.

12. THE DEVIL AND MICHAEL SCOT

The Faustian tale of a Scottish magician–polymath

PERSONS OF THE DRAMA

A young girl, daughter of Michael Scot
Geordie Bell
Tam Page (Wagner)
Michael Scot (Faust)
The Devil (Mephistopheles)
Three Judges, including the President of the Court
Troupe of Spirits in the forms of beautiful women,
including their image of Agatha (see below)
The Devil's imps
Agatha (Gretchen)

Names in brackets are of the roughly equivalent characters in Goethe's *Faust*.

This play's narrative draws on a scenario by Samuel Taylor Coleridge in his *Table Talk* (February 16,1833).

Performers should feel free to render the text in Scots. Linguistic and other improvisations are welcome. Within reason, this text isn't sacrosanct; have fun with it.

PROLOGUE

[Dusk. Stairs and balconies lit by candles, but a stranger and strong-er light comes from a high window at the right of the scene. This light shall wax and wane alternately, according to the mood of the action. A YOUNG GIRL is singing. She is unseen.]

YOUNG GIRL
> Why does a life bide on so long,
>> Michael, Michael?
> Why is an old man's heart so strong
>> Michael, Michael?
> Who dies in pain has lived for wrong
>> Or so to me they tell, o.
>
> They tell me of your dungeon look,
>> Michael, Michael;
> They cry down all that's in your book,
>> Michael, Michael.
> Who seeks the stone, is sure to brook
>> The brand of heaven or hell, o.
>
> But I shall calm the brand on your brow
>> Father, father,
> Renew my childhood kisses now,
>> Father, father.
> I'll dive so deep, they'll wonder how
>> You burst your centuries' cell, o.

[Descending one stair, at the left, and with amplitudes of noise and flesh: GEORDIE BELL. Ascending the other stair, at the right: TAM PAGE.]

58

GEORDIE BELL

Hic. Hey, Tam, Tam Page, is that you, man? Forty years and more am I here, and can I not just find my way through this maze. Hic. And yet, look, man, I can fairly jig on this stair ... just show me a lass, Tam Page, I'll be forty years younger and more. Uh oh, what's come to pass upby?

TAM PAGE

[now and then signalling for GEORDIE BELL to be quieter.] I can't ...

GEORDIE BELL

No, no, I can't either, though I've wandered the nether and the upper town, and there's not the nook thereabouts that doesn't serve you a nip without the crack and the cackle shaking the very lamps to laughter. Hic. Mind you, there's devil a lamp would know what it's laughing about, far less the folk themselves. No, no, I can't tell you either what all manner of gasbags and sweetie-wifes are saying about our own Sir Michael ... our own, and now everybody's own, Sir Michael.

TAM PAGE

Or nobody's.

GEORDIE BELL

Tam: Tam Page: Is he dead, then?

TAM PAGE

Nobody's, I meant, except his daughter's, or the devil's.

GEORDIE BELL:

> Tam ... Tam ... I'll tell you ... I'll tell you this,
> though,
> I dandered into that pub deep in the Cowgate,
> Not knowing just where I was. Tam, here, I'll tell
> you,
> It's such a while back, I'm damned if I remember
> Its very name ... Well, there I was, God's honour,
> Just a few choice folk in a place that once was
> hotching
> – Remember it, Tam – well, Tam, his table was
> empty
> Where our Michael ruled his students, his disciples,
> Boozers and hangers-on, you'll mind the crowd in
> that cellar
> Would draw itself to the rareness of that voice –
> Well, when I'm there just past,
> There's a sudden hush on the few poor drinkers
> there,
> For then – and mind, that place is far from sunlight –
> A thousand specks of dust danced in a beam
> That shot to our Sir Michael's sometime seat,
> And then – I'll tell you this, no word of a lie –
> Such shining grace, from heaven, dwindled to fog
> Thicker than winter mornings on the Firth,
> A fog that hovered over that rough-carved throne
> Then formed itself to a figure ... vanished ...
> vanished ...
> No, no, it can't be, no. I must be blethering.
> It's the drink talking, Tam.

[GEORDIE *quivers, in a cold sweat.* TAM PAGE *has
listened to all this impassively*]

TAM PAGE

> I can tell *that*. But I can't tell more.
> Even I can't gain entrance to his bedside. I must wait
> for word here.

GEORDIE BELL

> Even you, Tam? Hic.
> But you were always his fellow-wanderer,
> His compañero in Spain and Sicily,
> Keeping him steady even in Paree
> When he was no more than a gormless laddie,
> When libraries would weary even him
> And bottles beckon, or his teenage blood
> Fermented by some fly and buxom
> Bonnebonne of the Sorbonne;
> You guarded him from all that.
> Yes man, Tam Page, he's in your debt. He is that.
> Hic.

TAM PAGE *[irritated.]*

> So you say.

GEORDIE BELL

> Ay, a deep laddie, our wee Mike. Hic.
> Still is too. Youse were well-suited.
> I can see you, Tam, though I wasn't there.
> (Well, an ignorant body the like of me
> Wouldn't be there then, would he?)
> Always Tam Page at the side of Michael Scot,
> His partisan in scholarly dispute
> (Or whatever you call it),
> His research assistant, librarian,

As well as his best professor and tutor-body,
At once his aide-de-camp and general.

TAM PAGE *[more irritated]*
    Will you keep your voice down, man?
    My Michael's dying.

GEORDIE BELL
    Aw, Tam, Tam, I didn't mean ...

TAM PAGE
        Just shut it.
        I'm going up. Maybe they'll let me in.

*[Knocks at the door – in vain. Descends a few steps. GEORDIE
BELL nervously clutches a railing: he can never keep still, and con-
tinues to splutter. TAM looks up at the window, whose light lessens,
as if a candle had been extinguished.*

*He waves at GEORDIE for to go away. GEORDIE shakes with
fear, then wobbles off as fast as his weight will let him.*

*Another candle is put out. TAM ascends a few steps. A few sec-
onds, and the window is completely dark. THE YOUNG GIRL
emerges from the door: with a faint smile she recognises TAM: the
two meet in a comforting embrace. She descends to stage level and
faces the audience. TAM bows his head]*

YOUNG GIRL
    My father, Sir Michael Scot, dissolves into the
        elements.
    He who would yoke together the things of matter
        and spirit

Is himself sundered.
After the strivings of his life, and the strivings of his
     dying,
How calm was the death itself.
For others' faiths, he came to have respect,
And visiting a church, removed his cap –
A stone dislodged from the roof and struck his
     forehead.
It was as if he welcomed death with that gesture,
Courteous at the last. Ah, but when death approached
     him,
They were strong spirits the two, they had to fight;
To know the ways of dying, was for father
The final study, and by far the toughest.
 With what flourish, with what grace,
'My work is done,' he said; 'I have found the stone.'
There was a last light on his broken face.
I held him close, and he was gone.

[Music – The Flouers o the Forest]

ACT ONE

[The window in the Prologue is now that of a prison cell, with bars. MICHAEL SCOT is alone here. The only lights come through the window and from a candle on the cell table. In this Act, especial use should be made of silences, sometimes suggested in the text by three dots.]

MICHAEL

Betrayed! Betrayed! Betrayed! *[crescendo]*
There you are, Michael – and by your own people
That you came back for.

[smashes a plate against the wall of the cell, then calms down a little ...]

Ah, Michael, see yourself now.
See yourself, though no looking-glass
Is provided by the prison authorities.
Your only looking-glass is your own soul
And the memory of envious eyes.
Your long years of questioning,
And reverence for questioning,
This then is your answer.

[Gestures round the enclosed space.]

Hélas, Michael, the people of Scotland
Prefer reverence without questioning.
Michael, you acted on your knowledge,
Aiming the action for the people,
Too piously, it seems! The people of Scotland

Prefer piety sans action.
Europe for learning, Scotland for girning! The people
        of Scotland:
I can't call them the Scottish people –
That phrase implies a unity that's wanting.
They're the phantom people of a former nation,
They're drizzle through a cemetery
That leaves the soil and stone as sterile dry ...
Phantoms! And I'm the palest ghost of all:
Fourteen years in here have taken my youth;
– Or should I blame, in truth,
My travels? No ... it's being fastened here
In a Scottish jail,
Has torn me from my land while *in* my land;
Time, more than space, estranges ... Yet this ghost
Can't make it through such walls ... Here, with what
        stones
Have they built this place? I know. Each stone
        around me
Was once a Scottish heart.

[Feels round the wall with his hands.]

Time estranges me from myself, my elements split
        from each other,
All that I brought together in myself through my
        studies and my wanderings.
In Bologna, law; in Sicily, medicine; in Toledo ...
        alchemy...
A jail in Scotland crushes my works – and myself – to
        powder.
My sole consolation is this,

That a storm can no more penetrate these walls than I
      can penetrate them,
To blow my gatherings to every part.
To every part ... yet that was my ambition,
A 'lad of parts' (according to our phrase)
From the very edge of a Scottish country town
Spreading his knowledge through the universe
Bearing honour to himself, his family,
His nation ... sharing its wealth with other nations ...
– My nation holds a meaner sense of wealth:
It scatters itself all-roads for baser metals,
Like cankered mice that skelter down the alleys,
Losing themselves in a maze
All for to nab the single prize of the chase,
A hunk of mouldy cheese for rotten teeth.
[Much bitter gesturing.]

Scotland, and I, are all crumbled away.
How unlike this building! Oh yes, let's dissolve
      what's best in ourselves,
But keep intact our jails! That's my country all over ...

[A sequence of harsh music, counterpointed by a steadily growing light on the stage. Light and dark should alternate for a while to suggest the passage of days. MICHAEL is now and then seen to be pressed against the walls, either sliding along them in despair or trying hopelessly to dislodge even a fragment of the stonework. At last, a stone moves, very slightly at first but it becomes gradually looser. MICHAEL is able to remove it, likewise its neighbour and so on, until there's a hole big enough to get through. Sudden, blinding, flashes of light (obliterating the window), until the stage is extremely bright, dominated by the upright, triumphant figure of MICHAEL.]

For the very first time in his life, Michael Scot is free!
Yes, that's what I said ... For the very first time in his
        life?
It wasn't life before – whether closeted
In a study or a jail ... now, Michael, your life begins:
Learn to live, man! But spin right back again
No doctor now, but a crawling baby
With walking, speaking, loving yet to learn –
Loving, did I say? So whom should I be loving?
Whoever brought their comfort to my cell?
– The rest of humanity can go to hell!

[A rumbling sound. MICHAEL *seems to shake, as if there
had been a tremor of the earth.]*

Freedom, freedom! But Michael can't be free
Of the will to strive. Michael without his thoughts,
His calculations and his explorations,
Recording all in volume after volume –
Michael then is no more himself, but a doll
Its paint peeled off, decaying, foppish, idle,
Of use but for firewood.

*[The lighting at this point should suggest fire, then the stage gradu-
ally darkens. Music. The window reappears, this time with a Gothic
arch.* MICHAEL *busies himself, hauling first a desk on to the stage
from the wings, then bookshelves and books. Lastly he retrieves a
globe and a skull, gazing at each in turn for a while, then places
them carefully on the desk. He sits on the desk, seemingly casually,
and again takes up the globe and the skull in each hand, as if bal-
ancing the one against the other.]*

This is the competition of the stones.
One would be bigger and heavier than the other.

[Brings them together with a knock. Laughs.]

See them trying to occupy the same space.
A cosmic game of bowls.
The Scots play bowls on grass well-manicured,
The French, on any flattish patch of gravel.
Michael plays bowls upon infinity …
That's good enough for him. Michael disowns
Lesser competition than of these stones.

[Makes the knocking-together gesture again and laughs, this time in a weirder manner. Further suggestion of tremors and fire. MICHAEL takes up a book from the desk and reads.]

Huh! It's my own production, this,
– Written long syne.
Can the young man I was
Teach the old boy I am
With a single line
Wrought here in eagerness unhid,
Though slavering audience undid
The dense and subtle knot of words,
Then laced it loose for men in black
To trip and land me on my back?

[Shakes the book.]

Me! Guilty of … magic!
Me, condemned for what I condemned myself:

I was always against the misuse of my findings.
But a lonely scholar who loves company...
Yet another proffered cup, and his tongue over-free ...
Ignoring old friends who gestured their fears,
I poured the right discourse into the wrong ears.

[THE DEVIL appears, just below the Gothic window. MICHAEL looks up with an expression of self-reproach (and self-pity). He reads from the book.]

'A vain and innocent teacher at his ease
Falls for his worldly pupils' flatteries.'
– If only I'd followed my own advice.

[Slams the book shut. Three JUDGES, draped and hooded in black, appear at the study, to the left; that means they're in line with THE DEVIL at the right.]

Then came my judgment, and the proclamation
Posted at every town-square in the nation.

[The second of the judges, THE PRESIDENT OF THE COURT, steps forward and reads from a scroll.]

THE PRESIDENT OF THE COURT
*IT IS DECREED THAT THE SAID MICHAEL
SCOT
DENOUNCED BEFORE THE TABLES OF OUR
LORD
BY CERTAIN JUST AND SOBER CITIZENS
HAVING HEARD FROM THIS UNHOLY
HERETIC
OF HEATHEN NOTIONS LEARNED IN GODLESS
PARTS.*

IT IS DECREED THAT THE SAID MICHAEL
SCOT
SUFFER THE DUE PROCESS OF DESERVED
CONFINEMENT
BOTH SOLITARY AND PERPETUAL
AND THE LORD DARE NOT HAVE MERCY ON
HIS SOUL.

*[*THE PRESIDENT *steps backwards. All three* JUDGES *disappear as the stage darkens to the left. To the right, the light through the window grows redder, as does the figure of* THE DEVIL. MICHAEL *takes up his book again.]*

MICHAEL
Well, here's *my* words again.
Four things, I say, make a man wise.
One: INTELLIGENCE OF REASON.
--- For sure: Pity I forgot about *emotion,*
others', and my own.
Two: DILIGENCE IN DOING.
--- Fine, but you've got to stop and take a
look at yourself, then burst out laughing.
Three: EXPERIENCE OR KNOWLEDGE.
--- 'Experience' by itself would have served
me better.
Four: A LIVING MEMORY.
--- You're not going to easily forget fourteen
years in the nick.

*[*THE DEVIL *steps forward. He speaks affectedly, now and then with a hint of self-conscious vulgarity, as if this arch-aristocrat felt a need to parody the common touch.]*

THE DEVIL
>Nick? Old Nick? Did I hear my name? At your service.

MICHAEL
>*[somewhat engrossed, doesn't pick up* THE DEVIL's *utterance; he reads on.]*
>'Knowledge Can serve three ends:
>>*One:* KNOWLEDGE can serve KNOWLEDGE itself.
>>*Two:* KNOWLEDGE can serve POWER.
>>*Three*: KNOWLEDGE can serve LOVE.'

>*[Reads on, muttering.]*

>'Let us expand on the third. KNOWLEDGE can serve LOVE.
>LOVE OF ANOTHER PERSON ...'

>*[Picks up the skull and addresses it.]*

>That's you, pal.
>'And LOVE OF THE LAND ...'

>*[Picks up the globe and addresses it.]*

>And that's you, Scotland. You're there ... hereabouts. Fine, all this, but look where love of the people and of my country got me: Never mind, I can still be gentle with you both.

>*[Mockingly, he kisses first the skull, then the globe, then knocks them together. He laughs demonically.]*

THE DEVIL

Setting up as a scholar again, I see:

MICHAEL

Who the hell are you?

THE DEVIL

Who *out* of hell would be more accurate. But I shouldn't speak so to Michael Scot. It would be awfully pedantic if not presumptuous.

MICHAEL

You don't know me, pal.

THE DEVIL

I know you better than you know yourself.

MICHAEL *[sighing.]*

Ay, you're maybe right there. Just before you appeared, I was only *beginning* to know myself.

THE DEVIL

I could help with the process. Mind you, if you'd called me earlier, you'd have had a lot more fun in your young days – or, if you hadn't wanted that, I could at least have got you out of a few scrapes.

MICHAEL

Such as?

THE DEVIL

Fourteen years in the slammer, for one thing. I could have swung things your way on the religious court.

No bother at all – with my influence. If only I'd been asked. Besides, it wouldn't just have been a case of getting you out of situations but also into them.

MICHAEL

What are you going on about?

THE DEVIL

Take that job you were after. Archbishop of Glasgow. You had a foot in the door. The Pope gave you a testimonial. I could have given you another. Again, you only needed to ask. Mind you, I was half-tempted to apply for the job myself.

MICHAEL

I'll not deny I was disappointed not to get it. It would have been a timely sinecure. I still had a pile of manuscripts to get through – alchemy, astrology, mathematics, medicine – you name it. I could have translated the lot in no time ...

THE DEVIL

And I could have looked after the cathedral and the diocese for you. I mean, I know the Glaswegians; they're my own flesh and blood. Name me any city of virtue – it's fertile territory for your humble servant. *[Points to himself and bows mockingly.]*

MICHAEL

No doubt ... but what brings you here just now?

THE DEVIL

You called me, Michael.

MICHAEL
    No I didn't.

THE DEVIL
    You did.

MICHAEL
    Didn't.

THE DEVIL
    Did.

MICHAEL
    Didn't.

THE DEVIL
    Did.

MICHAEL
    All right, you win. We can't go on like a couple of
    bairns. Since you're here, we've got serious work to
    do. Or rather *you've* got serious work to do.

THE DEVIL
    'We' ... 'You ...' *Qu'est-ce que c'est la différence?* You're
    in me and I'm in you.

MICHAEL *[laughing.]*
    You're maybe right there, after all, but you put it
    in an unprofessionally speculative manner. A good
    scholar has to back up his assertions with evidence.

THE DEVIL

>Oh, I'm as good a scholar as you. No doubt about it. So, it's better we work together rather than compete for the best jobs. We've so much in common, Michael.

MICHAEL

>Ay, right!

THE DEVIL

>We're both intuitive types. I know you wanted me to come here long before *you* wanted me to come here.

MICHAEL

>Did I? ... *[Looks at the ground.]* Anyway, what's all this about 'intuitive types'? Evidence, evidence!

THE DEVIL

>We're both musical. It's well known that I'm a virtuoso on the fiddle. Whenever I take human form, I've got to support myself somehow ... I take bookings for stag nights, hen nights, weddings, funerals ... I've had gigs at the Edinburgh Folk Club. All in all a nice wee earner ... you know that. OK, the fiddle wasn't your instrument, but ... you know that kind of life.

MICHAEL

>I've known it from my earliest student days.
>Who's young, and knows the strings, who strolls and
>>plays
>From door to door, is guided well by his lyre.
>That was *my* instrument. No angels' choir

More eloquent, they said, than Michael Scot.
He, a poor scholar, strummed his way and bought
Many hours' learning
With one hour's earning.

[Smiles faintly, sighs heavily.]

That's it. I served my time with my lyre, and in turn
it served me with time.

THE DEVIL

As did these religious judges. Only your lyre didn't
give you fourteen years. Come on, Michael, all this
self-denial, has it been worth it?

MICHAEL

When it's been toughest, then I've had the most
          hope.
A country lad, from a large decaying family,
To be the greatest mind in Europe?
I couldn't afford not to take up the challenge. Listen.
I've a tale for you. This monkey had three bairns.
Hunters chased her through every wood in Africa.
Well, Madam Ape takes her favourite brat by the
          hand,
And tucks the second one under her arm.
What of the third? She likes it least of all,
Lets it drop to await the hunter's spear.
Aha! The fly wee bugger jumps on her back.
It's the one to escape when she loses hold of the
          others.

THE DEVIL AND MICHAEL SCOT PLAY

THE DEVIL
> Most applicable to me, the fallen angel
> Who always bounces back: It's a pretty dream
> You've just related. Like you, I've a fascination
> For the unconscious, and its interpretation.
>
> *[Looks ironically at* MICHAEL*]*
>
> That tale's in one of your books, just as you quote it.
> I read it in your soul before you wrote it.

MICHAEL
> *[Picks up the skull; gestures on it, in a manner suggested by
> the following speech.]*
> If you'd read further yet, you would have seen
> How I regard the subject in all its complexity –
> I've threaded a labyrinth too tangled even for a subtle
>   devil like you – or me:
> Thinkers will come after me who'll light the
>   scratchings on the human cavern
> In alcoves and interstices where I was the first to
>   fumble merely.
> I tell you, they'll have instruments with diamond
>   needles to trace the scratchings
> And the sound shall be an uncanny screech in the
>   night
> Echoing through the whole of a man or woman –
> The hidden pain no more ignorable –
> So I, the foremost reasoner of my time,
> Shall be the first to warn against unreason
> And few will want to know.

I dread the more that though my discoveries shall be
          refined by others,
In that age to come, even fewer will want to know.

THE DEVIL

    That'll mean even richer pickings for me!

MICHAEL

    Yes, I've no doubt of that: folk are the most
          unguarded
    When they've guarded themselves too well.

[Lays down the skull, gently and sadly.]

THE DEVIL

    You were extra-aphoristic just that minute.
    It's uncool ... though there's a certain charm in it.

MICHAEL

    [Half-singing, as in a dream, and as THE DEVIL *beck-
    ons to a* TROUPE OF SPIRITS, *who appear* IN THE
    FORMS OF BEAUTIFUL WOMEN, *and who dance
    before* MICHAEL. MICHAEL'*s dream state causes him
    to dance too.]*

    A young laddie dreams in his own manner;
    Newly become a man, he dreams anew.
    The greybeard dreams more differently still
    But a woman's dreams? Ah, there my science fails!

    [He tries to embrace one of the women, THE IMAGE OF
    AGATHA, *but she darts away from him; is followed by*

the others as she exits from the stage. MICHAEL *snaps out of his vision.]*

Hey, you devil of a devil, what did you do to me there?

THE DEVIL *[with mock-hurt-innocence.]*
Me? You must have been on the bevvy.

MICHAEL
There were women there!

THE DEVIL
Is that so? Probably just a few of my female staff. Poor darlings, it's hot work for them. They like to get out and about when they can – you know, go clubbing, on the prowl ...

MICHAEL
They were leading me on! And leading part of me above. *[Gestures at his crotch]*
One of them was anyway.
I don't want to revive old stirrings. Listen:

[Grips THE DEVIL *by the shoulders.]*

Three roads are hard for me to work out,
And a fourth thing ... well, I'd rather pass that by.
The first: the way of an eagle through the sky;
The second: the path of the serpent over the rocks;
The third: the course of a ship that's in mid-ocean ...
The fourth ... I can barely speak of it ...

– The manner of a human male in adolescence.
  [Fidgets absent-mindedly and nervously with the skull.]
I ... I ... was quoting Solomon. *[Naïvely]*

THE DEVIL

I've a lot of time for that chancer. Knew how to have
fun. Imagine if he'd written your books and you'd
written the Proverbs!

[Silence as they look at each other: THE DEVIL *as if he
was waiting for* MICHAEL *to make some big decision;*
MICHAEL *as if he wanted to say something but couldn't,
yet.]*

Michael, my old buddy, you're a sorry wee soul.

MICHAEL

A purchaseable soul, eh?

THE DEVIL

I was going to say that with your tormented look
You either talk from, or talk like, a book.

MICHAEL *[Grabbing* THE DEVIL *suddenly and violently.]*
TALK LIKE A BOOK? THEN MAKE ME ACT
LIKE A MAN!

*[Suddenly he realises the implications of what he's just said.
He shakes off* THE DEVIL, *who nevertheless approaches
him and grips his hand.]*

THE DEVIL AND MICHAEL SCOT PLAY

THE DEVIL

> You're on, friend: And from this very day
> The contract made (in the traditional way),
>
> *[Shakes MICHAEL's hand up and down, vigorously.]*
>
> By underworldly law we have elected
> To evolve yourself in ways you have neglected.
> I heard you when in jail and quite demented
> Complaining that your life was so fragmented!

MICHAEL

> *[now shaking THE DEVIL's hand up and down, and
> even more vigorously.]*
> Thus I abjure my former loyalties,
> Once slave to Scotland's futile worthiness!
> I have no fear of where I'll be gone
> A quarter-century on.
> To your domain I'll gladly pay all duties;
> It's warmer there, and free of goodie-goodies.

THE DEVIL

> You need no fear of where you'll be gone
> A quarter-century on.
> Down there, you have your fans ... and I'll attest
> A catch like Michael Scot's an honoured guest!
> *[Aside:]* (An honoured permanent guest, that is.)

MICHAEL

> My darkest yearnings I no longer hide –
> I'll join the infernal pantheon with pride:
> Secrets of earth which I have garnered dearly

To those of hell can now be grafted merely,
To raise a prickly stock that's not averse
To shake its leaves throughout the universe:
To my observatory!

[Brief business with the little globe: MICHAEL *chucks it
playfully from the one hand to the other.]*

Colleague, come!
Let Scotland stick its crawlies up its bum!

[Rude gesture with fist and arms, tongue rasping. The study vanishes in darkness; MICHAEL *and* THE DEVIL *are revealed on the
roof with a telescope:* MICHAEL *raises his arm and that of* THE
DEVIL, *their hands grasped as in the earlier vice. Stars appear.]*

I've read, I've written, I'll *live* the constellations!
I would be Aquila, soaring over nations;
Powers of brain transferred to beak and wing
And talons ever-poised to catch and cling.
See me as Draco, writhing out such fire
We alchemists desire of the elemental
For our great synthesis ... And there's the Lyre!

[Releases THE DEVIL's *hand.]*

Strings of my studenthood, and still as gentle ...

[His mood mellows in these last two lines.]

THE DEVIL *[pointing to the sky.]*
You wrote that planets are not so defined
Within their spheres, like frightened folk confined

Within their houses; – rather, you advanced
That they resembled spirited types who danced,
Laughed, and played sports through a long holiday
Beneath a canvas arching the public way.

MICHAEL *[also pointing to the sky.]*
The pleasure principle which my land forgot:
I theorised about it quite a lot.

[Raises both arms. THE DEVIL'S IMPS *appear and dance grotesquely around* MICHAEL*]*

Enough of blethering! The game's a bogy!
Michael no more's a fussy foosty fogy!

*[*THE IMPS *raise a mock-admiring hoot at this over-the-top alliteration.* THE DEVIL *jumps, arm and fist directed at the sky. Then total darkness and silence, followed by a series of dissonant chords. The barred window at the top right reappears, with flames crackling behind it. A light falls on the desk, and on the globe and skull, both still there but having now a presence that is somewhat pathetic.]*

CURTAIN
END OF ACT ONE

ENTR'ACTE

[A pub, deserted but for GEORDIE BELL, *who approaches a wooden chair built and carved in a Gothic style. He stares at it with some apprehension, but after a drop or two from his tankard, he tentatively touches it, feels it, as if doubtful of its reality. Then he sits on it, and beams at the audience with an expression of naïve confidence and good-natured smugness. Every so often he accompanies the following account with unctuous gestures. He appears to have learned it by heart, as from a book, and displays a provincial earnestness.]*

GEORDIE BELL

He was a scholar who ranged through all disciplines.
It was wondered how he later became a specialist
in hocus-pocus. Michael Scot and his secret powers
stirred up the continent. In every nation – except his
own – attention would be paid by the men of pow-
er. They were afraid of this northern wanderer, who
spoke as if he had gained his learning from a single
book. In every nation – except his own – he read the
stars with an unusual facility. This gave him the pow-
er to establish new relationships between phenomena:
astrology revealed analogy. By examining the rust on
a sword, he could diagnose the disease of the swords-
man. He analysed metals and men with such uncanny
perception, that people became curious about that
burnished glass through which he peered every night.

[GEORDIE clears his throat importantly, gets up from the chair, paces about, then, with a twinkle in his eye, returns to the chair and resumes.]

The King of France gave orders for a grand banquet and ball. He either feared or forgot to invite Michael. Michael, however, concluded that it had been palace policy not to have him along. The ladies there were all beautiful; Michael was offended. So he strides into the royal hall, just smiling; he hears the sudden fall of a silken silence. That throne can fairly shake.

[GEORDIE mimics this movement in the Gothic chair:]

Michael leads up his finest beast, a courser with such eyes that could lead its rider right through Hell. Its black coat shines in the candlelight.

[GEORDIE now mimics MICHAEL: he puts on a doctor's cap and gown similar to those worn by MICHAEL.]

'King, my friend,' declares Michael. 'I spy here a princess who'd prove a nice wee catch for me. Now, if I happened to become prince of your southern lands, I could be matched equally with her. My rule, let's say, could be absolute – and that would mean less work for you. Imagine, having Michael Scot as a relative and a colleague!

'Think it through. My horse here will stamp three times on your palace floor. Three times, that's all, as I wouldn't want to unsettle your delicate guests any further.'

[GEORDIE gets up, takes off the cap and gown, then returns to the Gothic chair.]

At the first stamp, the bells of France rang throughout the land. At the second, the towers of the palace fell to the ground. At the third stamp –

It never came. The King screamed out an oath: Michael should have his princess and his principality.

[GEORDIE leers, in a patronising manner.]

It's not long before our northerner is exhausted by all that lovemaking on a Mediterranean beach. He decides to suspend his exile for a while ... if that's all right with the princess and his other ladyfriends. He can't bear the heat of the sun (nor of Hell?)

So he rides and sails to Scotland incognito, to the cooler beaches of Fife. He was born near here. Every region except this one is witness to his fame.

[GEORDIE leaves the seat and performs the rest of the narrative with appropriate business: he has cap and gown in readiness.]

He seeks a stone that he knew well in his youth; it rises grimly above the marsh. Here, in the winter drizzle, glide the lonely pilgrims of the damned. This is the Bell Crag, a mass thrust up from Hell.

Michael rides to the top of the Bell Crag. Below, there extends a dell of broken and twisted trees; this forms a rough amphitheatre to his stage. Leaping about are imps and will-o'-the-wisps, scaring away the sheep and cattle.

[GEORDIE puts on the cap: drapes the gown over one shoulder. THE DEVIL'S IMPS from Act One reappear.]

Michael raises an arm, reins in his steed, addresses his audience: 'Hear me: You with your misshapen heads, your globe-like eyes, your leathery ears. This is my own land. It denounced my achievements and threw me in prison.

'It forgets me. I remember it. Only too well. We'll claim my due, since I am claimed by our good lord the Devil.'

[GEORDIE lays the cap and gown on the floor.]

The black courser heard out Michael to the end of his speech. It stamped the summit of the Bell Crag, and left the mark of its hoof.

[THE DEVIL'S IMPS disperse. GEORDIE winks and leaves the stage. Darkness, save for a spotlight on the cap and gown.]

ACT TWO

[Landscape. A ruined building, almost only one wall remaining, at the right; it has one window, positioned as in previous scenes, but this time it's no more than a gaping rectangle. AGATHA *and* TAM PAGE *approach the ruin.]*

AGATHA

> Ay, but I mind they told of the dungeon look
> Of a warlock nightly cowering in these stones.
> I mind my mother warning me that here
> I'd surely see the mould upon his bones.
>> Folk held that ghost in fear
>> For more than fourteen year.
>> Some said that he'd then vanished to his
>>> home
>> In Hell, as sudden as at first he'd come.
> Others denounced all that as lies:
> *Come on! He'll not return to his neuk –*
> *He's never left it!* Their grave heads shook.
> *This is his cell, they said, for centuries.*

[She gestures to the ruin.]

TAM PAGE

> I'm too old now to cry that down:
> Once I would call it country-folk's blethers.

AGATHA

> What changed you, master Tam?

88

TAM PAGE

> The years, love,
> And they're centuries enough for me, I'll tell you.

AGATHA

> There must have been a moment in these years,
> You recognised the flaw in the formula.

TAM PAGE

> I'm a sad practical man that's worked long,
> Then recognised he's won – and learned – nothing.

AGATHA

> If that were so, boss, I wouldn't be here.
> You learned me your skills, you who have pounded
>   powders
> To cure the sick in foreign lands, in the courts and
>   the streets across Europe –
> All this you passed on to one girl of a Scottish village.
> But that, even that, isn't enough. You know it.
> I need more than your learning: I need your
>   unflagging strength:
> Your patience and your hope.

TAM PAGE

> *[smiling, half at her expostulations and half at his*
> *memories]*
> *Bon courage!* That's what *he* said to me.

AGATHA

> Who?

TAM PAGE
> Your master's master.

AGATHA
> Doctor Michael Scot?

[MICHAEL SCOT *approaches feebly, somewhat stooped. His cap and a scarf obscure his face. He gradually removes these, but retains the black gown which seems to envelop him. He recognises AGA-THA as the embodiment of the spirit-woman whom he tried to embrace in Act One.]*

MICHAEL
> I have never heard such music in my name:
> It leads up through my clever-written scales,
> The lines I've drawn to fix a note on a star
> Me, arrogant, certain ... and deaf.

TAM PAGE
> *[with obvious delight at meeting MICHAEL.]*

> Deaf until now, both of us, Michael.

AGATHA
> *[gasps in astonishment. MICHAEL SCOT is revealed as a handsome young man.]*

> Michael ...

MICHAEL
> That's more harmonious yet – 'Michael' alone –
> Though Michael has indeed been alone too long.

TAM PAGE *[smiling.]*
> Alone,
> Bar devils and demons in that same employ
> That once was mine, before they jailed you, boy.

AGATHA
> Michael ...

MICHAEL
> And again! Though that sweet sound is undeserving
> To this curmudgeon ego. Yet, and yet,
> 'Michael', addressed as when he was a child,
> Here, at this spot ... my birthplace, at these stones ...

> *[gestures at the ruined tower.]*

> 'Michael' the name alone without the hooh-hah
> Of 'Doctor' – pah! The best of his knowledge now
> Is knowing there's so much he'll never know.
> Michael *'Scot?'* ... Hah! he who collected tongues
> (As others collected faces), he has forgotten
> The meaning of that one little word ... 'Scot'.

[MICHAEL removes the gown, drapes it carefully over the stones of the ruin. He seems to become more radiant – even younger in manner? – every time he sees AGATHA. In turn, TAM PAGE becomes infected by this new sprightliness.]

TAM PAGE
> *Bien sûr!* But you always went further than me.
> You were an alchemist, and sought the stone.
> All your experiments, as subtly moulded

By simple human hands, or as you'd tend
A tropical plant in your too-northern garden
That flourished spite Tam Page's disbelief.

MICHAEL

I was an alchemist, known throughout Europe.
But what of that?
You are a chemist, you remove pain
From ordinary folk in a small town.

TAM PAGE

Michael, it's more routine, than an ideal.
Repetitive thud of pestle in the mortar –
That's all I'm fit for.

MICHAEL

How can you say 'that's all'?
You're far from fair to this lassie – even insulting!
You've taught her that same work you claim to
      despise ...

[points to AGATHA, *then to* TAM.*]*

– A *machine*, like you? If so, she's well disguised!

*[*AGATHA *is much taken with all this banter, especially with* MI-CHAEL's *last remark.]*

TAM PAGE *[laughing.]*

Come on, Michael, we were once a pair
But you were for perfection. I couldn't follow you
      there.

MICHAEL

> Perfection? Perfection? Tam, could you never see
> 'Perfection' was never good enough for me?
> I wanted a paradox:
> The less-than-perfection that's yet more-than-
> > perfection.
>
> This country always wants everything fitted neat,
> Finished-like, and every problem beat.
> It grabs the shears to prune our native rowan:
> – But I would see that grow, and keep on growing.

TAM PAGE

> Michael, you're as intense as ever you were
> Long ago, in Paris. Do you mind that poem
> You composed in a tavern by the Rue Mouffetard?
> There's quite an echo of it in your speech.
> 'Perfection' – that word, in your breath,
> Always held your fascination – if not your faith.

MICHAEL

> *[remembering the poem, which he recites in a daydream,*
> *as if he were taken back to his Paris years. Music should*
> *accompany the poem, as a mélodrame.]*
>
> **No at some smaa perfection dae we ettle,**
> > **Ti fyke aboot the smitch on the diamant;**
> **No in some sacrit chaumer will we settle**
> > **Ti bield the bruckle petals o the plant.**
> **Oors is the wark that warsles lang ti apen**
> > **The gowden yetts that baurs us aa aroun,**
> **Oors is the wark that gars us aye be shapin**
> > **The tree-like temple risin fae the toun ...**

THE DEVIL
> [*appearing from behind the ruin, and clapping his hands.
> Meanwhile, overcome with emotion,* MICHAEL *and*
> TAM *embrace, and engage in lighthearted converse with
> Agatha. They seem not to notice* THE DEVIL, *who ad-
> dresses the audience.*]
> Bravo! That has a homely eloquence,
> But to a dude *comme moi,* just makes no sense.
> He scorns 'some small perfection' – it's inhuman –
> But smallest *im*perfection *I'll* find room in!
> Secret or open, when he's feeling dozy,
> I'll find that blemish, where I'll curl up cozy!
> I'll burrow through his chamber, flick my tongue:
> When he awakes, he'll know that he's been stung.
> His 'tree-like temple', symbol of pieties,
> Long-laboured in his mental nurseries –
> He'll smell it slimed and wormy with disease!
>
> [*to* MICHAEL]
>
> Sorry, dear Michael: there you're in full flow,
> And I barge in and interrupt you so.

MICHAEL
> To that the simple answer is, well, no:
> I've just begun, and I've got far to go.
>
> [*Gazes at* AGATHA, *then confronts* THE DEVIL:]
>
> You that pressured me to set
> Seeming impossible tasks,
> And wouldn't let me be

Until I challenged you: *Make rope from the sand,*
Along the eastern shore of my Scotland,
A rope that's strong enough to hang you well
And send you screaming back to Hell!
That fairly put you in a pet,
Ensuring my first victory:
I couldn't at that moment understand
It was the more beyond your might
For you to turn an earlier spectacle
Of teasing phantom women, soon in flight,
To someone here, who's more substantial.

*[indicates AGATHA, who seems both attracted to, and
exasperated by, MICHAEL.]*

TAM PAGE

Friend Devil, you seem far from intimate
With problems he and I've discussed of late.
Given two sides of a triangle – I'd maintain
'Twas a light task the third to ascertain.

[turns to MICHAEL]

Michael: you countered, *fine for geometry,*
But not for a science of humanity!
I thought: such a deduction's facile, lazy
Unusually for you. I thought you'd gone crazy.

MICHAEL *[eagerly]*

O Tam, I see it now: that quest for the unknown side
of the figure –
My mathematics had clutched me down into the

95

tunnel of a mountain,
That I was blinded and tangled into roots that grow
    from deeper roots and yet deeper into an
    imprisoning infinity;
O the illumination! The triangle! That first side's
    myself,
The second is this Devil,
And the third is ... *[Points to* AGATHA.*]*

AGATHA

That's such ingenious nonsense, my poor dear:
It's a woman, a woman, standing here.

THE DEVIL *[triumphant]*

She'll prove much more than quantifiable fact,
She'll be the toughest nut you've ever cracked.

TAM PAGE

[roughly pushes THE DEVIL *aside, then draws with chalk
on one of the larger stones of the ruin.]*
If there's a figure here
The base, it's clear,
Isn't Michael at all
But Agatha.
Let's say, for the sake of argument,
Michael strikes out from one end of the line;
It's simple now to finish this design.

[draws THE DEVIL*'s side of the triangle.]*

Why is the Devil's line to Agatha's sent,
Except to show that he's irrelevant?

*[MICHAEL and AGATHA look in amazement at each other.
TAM PAGE maintains an expression of pedantic solemnity.]*

THE DEVIL *[drily]*
>Michael, this Tam of yours, why he's some boy.
>Indeed, I wonder why, with such a paragon,
>You needed the likes of me in your employ.
>Clearly my services weren't such a bargain.
>He's got it all finished-like and fitted neat
>And me fairly beat.
>Tam, you old sinner, your Devil's in distress
>That you have so outdone him in finesse.

AGATHA
>Paragon indeed: and none of you know how!
>This town and its region owe more to my master
>>than to anyone else:
>And they don't know it either.
>O what a feat it was, my devil, that thunder down the
>>valley,
>When Michael commanded you to cut the great cleft
>>in the hill.

[She gestures toward the back of the stage]

>Picks and shovels clanging on the outcrops once
>>kissed by tribal worshippers,
>Pulleys and pails stretching from here to Hell and to
>>Heaven,
>Could not have gouged and stolen away our country
>>with such deft ill-will.
>I felt in the theft of these stones
>The chipping of my bones –

And yet, I've often confessed,
Like everyone hereabouts, I was impressed.
For better, or likely, worse,
It was no more our land, our primal nurse.
And yet we felt elated
She'd been so violated.

*[THE DEVIL, meanwhile, smirks much; MICHAEL is
writing with shame: TAM maintains his stolid mien.]*

And who was it, faced with such destruction,
Challenged our seduction,
Turned evil to good use? None other than – Tam.
Snow and bog and the crag-face
Rock-falls and the bracken
Had long obscured the routes to the hilltop farms,
That shepherds and townsfolk would rarely meet
Either on the summit or in the street,
Though each required the other. Who solves this? –
      Tam.
He juts his jaw, he glowers,
Up and down the steps to every house he strides,
Commands the menfolk to get up off their backsides
– And the women too – even the lovesick teens
Picking alternately their noses and the flowers –
This dourest of tyrants turns them into machines.
Roads they build between the town and the isolated
      steadings,
Springs they divert in their course – thanks to you,
      Devil!
Thanks to you, Michael!
You must wonder, both of you, why

Tam prosaically concerns himself with the water
supply:
Ah! Devil! Through you, our Michael's imagination
Converts his science to magic:
Tam, for his part, too practical to be tragic,
Converts it to engineering and irrigation.

TAM

No: my dear lass, you do Michael an injustice:
All my practice was based on his principles
That he taught me when I alone was his confidant,
In those high years of our togetherness.

THE DEVIL

Aha! But you're missing something. Your precious
slopes
Had long been messed up by that set of dopes –
Your darling townsfolk! Tam, so you say, sets the task
And they prove heroes. But, *chers amis,* I ask,
If Mike and I were the *first* villains? Sorry,
You talk of the cleft; but you forget – that quarry!
It scarred the land before *our* enterprise.
Come on! The quarry. Where are your memories?

MICHAEL

Devil, that's just what I'd expect to hear
From such a slicker, such a boulevardier.
Your metropolitan wit misfires, too late:
No dilettante proved so desperate.

[contemptuously]

Listen. I've never told you this before.
There is my tower. Through what was once a door
You'd enter this my birthplace.
[THE DEVIL makes a mocking gesture of boredom.]

                         Yes, you know that,
But there's more yet. Into my father's estate
This tower, its lands, came with my mother's hand –
But first into decay, fell the marriage itself.
In the village it was said
That if old Scot should Balwearie's daughter wed
Their wealth and their children would be accursed.
By a village woman I was nursed
Who told me tales of predetermined ills,
And of my own random inheritance:
– Yet there was a spirit in her set me at defiance!
Her demons challenged my imagination and my will.
The tower's library lacked forbidden texts,
So this child wrote his own, and relieved his
                loneliness.
Young Michael Scot, born into downgoing gentry,
Pictured worlds in the evening smoke, and desired
                entry!

THE DEVIL
Your autobio, though touching, reeks of unction.
We made a deal, twenty-four years ago,
And you can't plead grounds of family dysfunction;
Nor can your obligations be dismissed
Through your being a premature existentialist.
      Now I'm running short of rhyme,
         So come on, kiddo,
            It's burny-burny time.

MICHAEL
> Kiddo! Well, well, indeed I could tell you how
> I've never felt as young as I do now.
> Though you gave me elixirs, enabling me to prance
> Right up the skirts of that poor princess of France –

[stops, embarrassed, at a glance from AGATHA.]

> I've no more illusions about myself, or your powers,
>> or about these lands and townships of
>> Balwearie,
> The decline of this clan of Scots, the internecine
>> acrimonies
> Fathers against sons, husbands against wives, brothers
>> against brothers –
> Our folk quick to follow the cold money men who
>> saw the gap, and stepped in,
> Quarried the hill and built the mill out of it –
> The craftiest among them enslaving the others.
> Such subtle dominion was new in this our glen,
> No Scot, no Balwearie, had wielded as much as these
>> men!
> Ah, yes, the quarry – and you reproach *me* with *that!*
> I might have been proud of such, initially,
> But not for long. There was stone for the mill, for
>> granaries,
> For walls against floods and landslides, for viaduct
>> causeways, statues to our 'worthy
>> benefactors' and all the rest of it,
> Stones, too, for homes where you'd scorn to crouch
>> down and shit:
> But the somnolence of our people is endemic;

They bore with the filth, and the ultimate epidemic.
Those who survived wandered pallidly around the
        town, bleating and stumbling
On the nettles that spread through the cobblestones,
        mumbling
As they carried the dying children to the common
        pit.
By then, to boot,
Our lords had made off to the cities with their loot.

THE DEVIL
    Come on, cram it all in:
    No doubt this caused you to study medicine.
    You know, it seems, my influence on events
    Better than I myself! Crimes, accidents,
    Blame them all on the Devil! I fear I've been much
        too pliable:
    Rather than claim men's souls, I should sue them for
        libel.
    Come on, Sir Michael, I've really had my fill:
    Admit you bullied me into splitting that hill.
    You hated the quarry that turned men into stone,
    And so, perversely, you wanted to cut your own.
    It was an act of scorn and vengeance
    Stabbing the country that treated you with
        indifference:
    No other nation in Europe would ever fail
    To honour you, but Scotland slung you in jail.
    Fourteen years! I felt for you, my brother;
    So I helped you settle one old SCORE with another!

[laughs somewhat hollowly as he points to the cleft.]

MICHAEL

> Unfortunately, you're now forgetting
>> That the second, unlike the first cut,
> Avoided blood-letting:
>> I was angry, but
> This land was still my land
> This folk was still my folk.

THE DEVIL *[with mock innocence]*

> By this sermon we learn
>> How a saint corrupts the Devil:
> Wishing evil, *he* effects good;
>> *I* wish good, and effect evil.

> *[AGATHA approaches MICHAEL; she seems about to
> take his hand: he glances at her. They are not yet ready for
> intimate gestures.]*

MICHAEL

> Mine was an act of scorn and vengeance, it's true, but
>> an act also of memory;
> An act against some of my folk, but not against all,
> A memory against a foul legacy,
> For a legacy bears all three parts of time
> Past, present, future – uniting in turn in memory,
> That nurtures saplings from the fallen trunk
> Where the spring gurgles through the bleached rock.
> A slime had spread itself all over Scotland,
> Where most slipped or stuck – but a few turned slime
>> to gold,
> That few so eager to sign the condemnation
> Of such a heretic as Michael Scot.

I wondered long, if I could burst through this ordure:
Would I not shrink to a flea, the more to infest
A country shrivelled to a verminous nest?
Quarries and canals – such small-town pettiness!
I would no longer be confined in a Scottish cell:
O for oceans and ships, the breezes bearing my
        sciences well,
While my country festers in its own mess.

AGATHA
    Michael!

MICHAEL
    I wandered long. I had a home, dear lady,
    Everywhere and nowhere. The dial of my soul,
    Swinging and quivering to the opposite pole,
    Where the pink-bathing South called out to me.
    So I forsook the burdensome cloak of Scotland,
    Under the spangling leaves, the crimson blossoms,
    The open cage of a Mediterranean trellis
    Where I loved a little, and learned much.
    Once, alone, I followed a coastal path
    Winding and dipping russetly between aloes and
        artichokes,
    To the naked rock of a templed promontory.
    I laughed my dancing thanks to Apollo and Dionysus,
    Through columns and capitals to the turquoise wine
        of the infinite.
    There came to me then a little peasant girl,
    Offering me a clump of lavender:
    I kissed and blessed it with my tears,
    Such tears as I had never wept before.

O I should have borne such a child on my empty
       back,
Lightly running with her to the summit of the vines.

[AGATHA looks more tenderly at him. and comes nearer.]

But I followed another course,
Conducting experiments at the castle in Naples,
Weights and balances over the trembles from Vesu-
vius;
Translating medical texts left by the Arabs
In flight from Toledo: the blood pulsed once again
Through that parched, parchmented city: bone would
       sing!
There you have me, Agatha,
I've achieved less than everything,
And on the way
To my work of healing
I've caused much pain.

AGATHA
But your land was still your land,
And your folk was still your folk.
It was both less and more than everything,
When you cleft the hill in two:
Anger led to beneficence.
The quarry, before you,
Bred only pestilence:
The going down of the children and the rising of the
      smoke
Must forever be remembered and redeemed,
So in answer to that blast, you carried a brand,

105

That candle-like on sickened hearts has gleamed:
We can never repair the first cut's devastation,
But the second cut still works regeneration.

[She takes MICHAEL'*s hand.]*

THE DEVIL
And I, *hélas,* have noted
That I've been ignominiously demoted.
Human beings have proved so vile,
That I'm now no more than the spirit of mere denial.
Though – unlike them – I can't be so destructive,
At least I can be stylishly reductive.
People need no bowels of an external Hell,
When their own nasty bowels can shit so well.

TAM *[shoving* THE DEVIL *aside.]*
Michael the alchemist sought the philosopher's stone,
And now he's found a jewel of his own.

*[*MICHAEL *and* AGATHA *kiss.* THE DEVIL *shows
signs of impatience.* TAM *tries to restrain him. Desperate,*
THE DEVIL *tries to grab* TAM *and lead him away.*
AGATHA *wrenches* TAM *free.* MICHAEL *pins* THE
DEVIL *against the wall of the ruin.]*

AGATHA
*[approaching the diagram, taking the chalk, and continu-
ing, against a musical accompaniment:]*
The corners of the triangle
Can be named at this last stage:

Michael Scot, myself,
And – Tam Page.

[She rubs out 'DEVIL' and inserts 'TAM P.']

THE DEVIL *[completely deprived of his customary poise.]*
All right. You win. I'm outsmarted – me! I release you
from your contract.

*[He makes a gesture of cancellation: arms in front, crossed
and uncrossed. His irony, which never leaves him, has
become bitter.]*

After this, anything's easy. Even making rope out of
sand. I reckon I'll take that up again, even hire you to
teach me.

MICHAEL
Fine! On one condition: that *you* make a pact with
me. I'd make damn sure I got *your* soul at the end of
the period.

THE DEVIL
For all you know, you and your successors might
possess my soul already.

*[THE DEVIL stamps three times on the ground. The others watch
in some dumbfounderment. Red smoke and light pervade the right of
the stage. At the third stamp, THE DEVIL vanishes.]*

CURTAIN
END OF ACT TWO

EPILOGUE

[Scene as in the Prologue, except that the desk from Act One reappears, with skull and globe. Stairs and balconies are again lit by candles. The window at the right, however, remains unlit.]

TAM PAGE
    Off Edinburgh's High Street
    At the corner of a close,
    Agatha with Michael Scot
    Set up house.
    I kept a chemist's shop,
    And when I put the shutters up
    We three would carry out experiments
    Upon the elements.
    My customers had no suspicion
    How Michael's erudition,
    Blended with Agatha's and my good sense,
    Made defiant advance
    Against stubborn ignorance.
    We were accustomed to bide our time.

    I'll set you a riddle.
    We three became ... four,
    Then once again three:
    Now we're two –
    Just one, when I die.
    I'd better explain!
    Agatha gave birth
    To a rare wee quine:
    The daughter, flourishing;

The mother, in decline.
One day, we find the shop
A heap of glass and dust –
Old enemies of Michael
Had burst through the lab,
Left his medicines impure
So his wife's beyond cure.
Michael and I were that heartsore
We deepened our learning all the more.
We were accustomed to bide our time.

The lassie grew
The make of her mother
Her father was her tutor
And I was another.
Where he misbuilt,
She'll design anew;
What he neglected
She'll see right through.
The blue of the sky's on her brow,
The wind in her breath;
For Michael Scot's daughter
Defeats his death.
A dynasty can bide its time.

His reasoning was supple:
Mine was – hah! – too lumpened.
Where I'd invent a mixture,
He'd come up with a compound.
In letters, by analogy,
His writing was as nimble:

I'd illustrate by allegory –
He'd discover a symbol.
Its meaning's beyond Tam Page's rhyme;
If you'd seek the stone, you must bide your time.

[TAM leaves the stage, to the left. More light falls on the desk. THE YOUNG GIRL enters from the right, takes up the skull and the globe, holds them to her bosom, and exits left. Less light on the desk. At last the window at the top right reappears: shimmering with strong red gleams, like fire. THE DEVIL's head is seen at the window. He starts to cackle, in the full force of his weird mockery.

Musical instruments, dominated by the fiddle, give out a few bars of intense dissonance, then suddenly stop. Complete darkness.]

CURTAIN
END OF PLAY

13. A TESTAMENT OF FIFE – SIXTH PART. KINGHORN TO HAWKCRAIG

Kinghorn's man of ideas we may know
In a man of art: sculptor Kenny Munro;

Burntisland shipyard-workers, rendered proud,
Dignified in labour, by painter-dialectician
Of gentle strength, the late Ian McLeod:
Unity of content with composition.

Macbeth, staged on Inchcolm! Yet, too, the expanse
Of coast and sea would set off Ariel's dance
In *The Tempest:* Hawkcraig Point's the place to go
For the magic landscape of Fife's Prospero:

DEPARTURE FROM THE ISLAND
(The Tempest)

Strange for a man who changes lands for lands
To ramble round that cove where the waves first laid
      him,
To clamber over kelp, slip down the sands,
Seeking a ledge that once in moonlight saved him:
Hoisting himself boyishly upon the brow
      Of that stone face he resembles now.

Has he a daughter's burgeonings to come,
Will set his few remaining books aside?

His briny invocations, and the hum
Of light-winged answers, glinting with the tide:
Not treachery, but love, dissolves his rule,
        Turns magus to time's fool.

Time's full for this same lord of Providence:
Spinning his webs of wiry gossamer,
Caught in the knot of his own vengeance
As briars bleed the miry sea-creature —
May not that inmate of a fouler cell
        Strike finer chords as well?

The diminution of our man's domain
Forced him to study herb, berry and spell,
To forage beneath hawthorn, so to gain
Dark drops of knowing; even the bluebell,
And golden scented gorse, yielded their story
        To the king of this promontory.

The cavern of his bitter alchemy,
The parapet of his too anxious pace,
The high-slabbed throne from where he princed the sea
And nurtured but one remnant of his race:
Here he dissolves at last the sweat and the dung
        Of his enemies' young.

His folk remark an antic voyager
Embark with them upon his ducal course:
So he distils a final elixir
Jigging on deck, while steadying to his source,
To clown in a castello by the lake
        For a grandchild's sake.

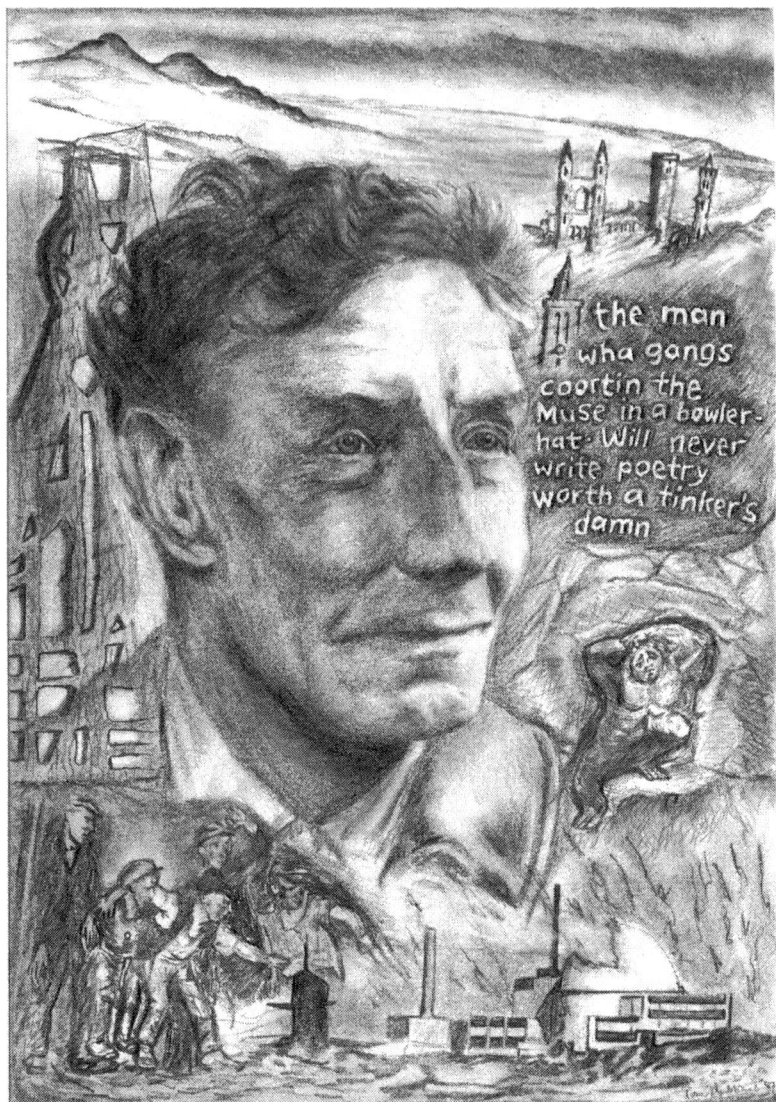

the man
wha gangs
coortin the
Muse in a bowler-
hat Will never
write poetry
worth a tinker's
damn

14. FIFE'S FOLK CULTURE, PAST AND PRESENT: JOE CORRIE (1894-1968) AND THE BOWHILL PLAYERS

There are books which, discovered when you are young, remain a moral and artistic compass for you throughout your lifetime.

In 1973 I bought a copy of *The Penguin Book of Socialist Verse*, edited by Alan Bold, and was intrigued by the presence there of a Scottish poet and dramatist called Joe Corrie. Alan's selection was small – four pages in all – but powerful. He included the longish poem 'Women are waiting tonight', on the aftermath of an 'accident' at the pit with multiple 'fatalities' (my inverted commas round these words are doubtless advisable):

> They will wait and watch till the dawn,
> Till the wheels begin to revolve,
> And the men whom they loved so well,
> The strong, kind, loving men,
> Are brought up in canvas sheets,
> To be identified by a watch,
> Or a button,
> Or, perhaps, only a wish.
> And three days from now,
> They will all be buried together,
> In one big hole in the earth.

The poem goes on to condemn the hypocrisy and crocodile tears of the establishment members who turn up at the funeral, of those such as the MP 'who voted that the military be used / When last these miners came on strike / To earn a living wage', the pit owner who 'vowed many a time / That he would make the miner eat grass', and also the right-wing press which had thundered against the strikers but who now squeeze every last drop of phoney pathos on to their pages. In due course, they will return to their usual function of 'storing up their venom and their hatred, / For the next big miners' strike.'

Alan Bold's biographical notes take up less than two lines: one suspects that at the time of the anthology's publication (1970), the editor had little to go on, as Corrie's life and work had receded into obscurity. However, in 1977, I learned that Joe Corrie had been active as miner and writer in my native Fife. Both my grandfathers had been down the pit. So I consulted the local collection in Kirkcaldy public library and copied by hand a good number of the poems appearing in the rare pamphlets published during Corrie's lifetime.

Fast forward seven years and Thatcher was at her height, determined to hammer once and for all those uppity enough to challenge her ideology. The miners went on strike and her response was ruthless and, it turned out, terminal – not for her, but for her adversaries. It was time for Joe Corrie to come into his own, and almost suddenly the revival got under way. The 7:84 Theatre Company toured Scotland with Corrie's now best-known play *In Time O' Strife*, directed by David Hayman, and Linda Mackenney brought out her book-length selection *Joe Corrie: Plays, Poems and Theatre Writings* (7:84 Publications, 1985). *In Time O' Strife* is set in a Fife mining community during the General Strike of 1926: it was electrifying to hear working-class Fife speech within the plush setting of Edinburgh's Royal Lyceum, in a kind of Brechtian dialectic of the familiar and the strange.

Around the same time, my friend William Hershaw and I served on the editorial board of a Fife-based magazine called *Scrievins* (Scots for 'writing'). We got the go-ahead to devote a special issue to Corrie. I drew a portrait, in pencil, of our author and that provided our image for the cover. The first article in the Corrie feature was by Alison Hutchison, who supplied a useful summary of Corrie's origins: 'Joe Corrie was neither a Fifer nor from a mining family. When the Corrie family moved to Cardenden in 1896 from Slamannan, near Falkirk, Joe was two years old. His father had been a grocer and his mother, before her marriage, had been a farm servant in Wigtonshire. [...] [T]his was a fairly common pattern in Cardenden at the beginning of the twentieth century. People came flooding into the area to work in the newly sunk Bowhill pit. Some of these came from exhausted pits elsewhere in central Scotland, but many of them had little or no experience of mining, they were just looking for work.'

Cardenden, located in central Fife, is now the collective name for a conglomeration of four former pit villages: from north to south (as also alphabetically), these are Auchterderran, Bowhill, the original Cardenden, and Dundonald. Though Joe Corrie would find himself in a vexed relationship with the conservative Scottish Community Drama Association, he had earlier enjoyed his collaboration with the Bowhill Players (later renamed the Fife Miner Players) who took *In Time O' Strife* on tour to many Scottish locations, with mostly working-class audiences. Lack of financial backing led to the demise of the company in 1931. During the leanest of times, the Bowhill Players supported their community in practical as well as artistic ways, notably by running soup kitchens, those ancestors of today's foodbanks.

Joe Corrie achieved a good measure of success in Germany, where his work was performed at Leipzig at the beginning of the 1930s, shortly before the Nazi takeover. My earlier allusion to Brecht might seem in keeping with this, but Corrie's more naturalistic aesthetic has led rather to comparisons with Zola (of *Germinal*) and Seán O'Casey, with regard, respectively, to the mining communities and to the staged domestic interiors.

The revivals over the past thirty-five years have served to compensate – amply – for the neglect of Corrie over the half-century or so from the early 1930s. William Hershaw and his fellow performers have created a new Bowhill Players who engage in many gigs across Fife and elsewhere in central-east Scotland. In a poignant gesture to the original bearers of the name, William's son David produced a CD which includes a re-issue of a 1929 Bowhill Players recording of Corrie's short comic play *The Miners' Saturday Night*, with the voices of Joe himself and his sister Violet. This, together with other tracks performed by today's Bowhill Players, is obtainable from <www.fraspublishing.co.uk≥ as an insert in the pamphlet *Joe Corrie: a Legend and his Legacy* by the late Scottish playwright Donald Campbell. A larger-scale production by our contemporary Bowhill Players is the CD *The Joe Corrie Project: Cage Load of Men*, complete with a booklet containing the texts and explanatory notes. The top-notch performances by the Players include such Corrie classics as 'It's Fine tae Keep in wi the Gaffer', a song which (to put it mildly) maintains its relevance in our own time:

> For mony a year I ha'e worked doon alow,
> But never in pits that are wet or are low,
> For I mak' it my business wherever I go,

> Aye tae keep in wi' the gaffer.
> Oh! it's fine tae keep in wi' the gaffer. [+ five more
> verses]

You hear this track and you could be forgiven for thinking
that the poem / song seems to have composed itself. It could
be mistaken for a folk song – but in a sense that's what it has
become: like Hamish Henderson's 'Freedom Come All Ye' it's
one of these radical Scottish songs that invite audience par-
ticipation.

> To order *The Joe Corrie Project* please visit
> <http://www.birnamcd.com>.

In some of his writings Joe Corrie expressed an understanda-
ble aversion to institutional religion. As a young student in the
early-mid 1970s I found myself looking to Russian literature
for clues as to how to retain a humane Christ-based ethic that
could blend with a socialist outlook. Initially I resorted to Tol-
stoy and that took me so far, but the stern simplifications of
his old age – as I discovered much later - jarred with the sub-
tle amplitude of his great novels, their ingenious structure or
'labyrinth of linkages'. Dostoevsky was a very different writer
but, again, his confused reactionary politics co-existed oddly
with the psychological and philosophical depth of *Crime and
Punishment.* (I would argue that Dostoevsky failed to under-
stand politics, but that he grasped the psychology of politics.)

At which point we may turn to Willie Hershaw's *The
Sair [Sore] Road* (Grace Note Publications, 2018) which
presents Jesus as a Fife miner, is structured according to the
Stations of the Cross, and which Derrick McClure has called
'one of the outstanding works of contemporary Scottish
literature'.

For Jim Aitken's extensive review of *The Sair Road* in *Culture Matters,* please go to <http://www.culturematters.org.uk/index.php/arts/poetry/item/3069-christ-is-a-communist-and-god-is-a-miner-the-sair-road-by-william-hershaw>.

I was struck by Jim's reference to the 'Grand Inquisitor' chapter in Dostoevsky's *Brothers Karamazov*. Here, Christ 'had been condemned by the Inquisition for giving us all the freedom to walk "the sair road" with all that implies for us.' The Grand Inquisitor puts it to Christ that people prefer security to freedom, and that the institution of the Church provides the former by infantilising the folk and guarding them from Christ's subversive offerings. It is not only the right wing who have interpreted this chapter as prophetic of Soviet totalitarianism, but it is the right which has made an industry of reducing Dostoevsky (as also Adam Smith) to crass homilies serving its own ideological purposes.

The irony latent in Jim's superb essay is that, in our own time, it is an authoritarian conservatism that values security over freedom, its media devoted to tacit if not covert propaganda and its middlebrow cultural products intended for passive, witless consumption. In contrast, Willie Hershaw and the Bowhill Players are reviving a Fife culture that was created *by* the folk and *for* the folk, both recording and animating its struggles, and giving new meaning in the twenty-first century as far-right conservatism elides into crypto-fascism, which becomes less crypto by the hour. Willie Hershaw and his brothers- and sisters-in-art offer the Sair Road's freedom over Inquisitorial security, or to use the parlance of our own time, they stand for hope over fear.

15. HAUF A KILT IN KELTY

In the late summer of 2005 I'd been on one of the hikes which are my antidote to what I'm doing now – writing. The northern boundary of the former Fife mining town of Kelty is also the county boundary: cross the burn, and you see the last remaining sign welcoming you to the old 'County of Kinross'. That burn once marked an ideological divide, at least as regards electoral cartography: south-central Fife, Labour (and on occasion Communist); Kinross, once the constituency of a Tory Prime Minister, Douglas-Home. In the Scottish Parliament of 2003-07, the Scottish National Party and the Liberal Democrats represented much of this landscape – though, curiously enough, the Communists (reformed as Democratic Leftists) still held seats on the local council.

Shifting party political allegiances must tell us something about the demography of a region, but not all: obviously folk don't think about party politics for most of their waking lives. During 2005's Westminster general election, the lamp-posts of Glasgow were festooned with placards: not so the lamp-posts of Fife. Call it Fife reticence, just getting on with life with the minimum of fuss. Not saying much but saying it with a near-silent eloquence. (A decade later, Fife people – a good many, anyway - would have become more obviously politicised.)

I'd come up the brae from the burn, back towards the cross-like intersection of Kelty's main streets, intent on a well-deserved pint of the black stuff. So I'm into the bar, don't know anyone there, wonder what my fellow-drinkers do for a living long after the pits have closed. I'm stood at the counter, waiting for my pint to settle. My red hold-all – a freebie from a Hungarian conference, and the one I take on hikes to carry maps, fruit and nuts – is resting on my rear. The bearded guy to my right looks at my bag and then at his mates: 'Here's a man wearin hauf [half] a kilt'.

I liked that welcome: part friendly, part mocking. Very Fife. It was an utterance that was certain to send my word-playfulness into overdrive. Here I am, wearing half of the national costume; I've been abroad a lot, and that has inevitably disturbed my relationship to my part of Scotland. Daft as it sounds, it can leave you feeling guilty – *Ah kept hauf o ma auld allegiances, hauf Ah kilt* [I kept half of my old allegiances, half I killed].

A year later, however, I was back in Hungary, and teaching Scottish literature at the Universities of Budapest and Pécs; the latter city is near the birthplace of Scotland's Saint Margaret, Queen and spouse of King Malcolm Canmore. During the mid-term break, and relaxing in Dunfermline, I picked up a batch of leaflets about Margaret, and on return to Pécs I gave these to my students. Young folk overseas are keen to learn about that little-known country called Scotland.

At the end of my Hungarian stint, and flying back to Edinburgh via Amsterdam, I looked down as the plane made its way over Loch Leven, Benarty, Lochore Meadows, Kelty and Cowdenbeath. I had a sudden rush of emotion and said to myself: I love Europe, and this is my country. At the time I didn't know that, ten years on, I would write a story – one of the three collected in my *Slavonic Dances* (Grace Note Publications, 2017) – set both in Scotland and central Europe, and that its title would be 'The Kilt'.

16. A TESTAMENT OF FIFE – SEVENTH PART. DUNFERMLINE

THE PROPHECY OF BANQUO
(King Malcolm's Tower, Dunfermline)

MACDUFF: [...] O Banquo, Banquo,
Our royal master's murdered.
LADY MACBETH: Woe, alas! What, in
our house?
BANQUO: Too cruel anywhere.
Macbeth, Act 2, Scene 3

When this is no more than a castle of bone,
The skull broken and the rictus forgotten;
When the crying has ceased from the maze of cells,
And the slaves who have breathed the winter-reek
anew
Shake their picks and their fetters in wariness of
freedom;
When the trunks have gnarled and twisted over the
earthbound walls,
And their branches have woven through gratings that
even now cling to abandoned passages;
Then you will visit this citadel for the last time
perhaps,
The chimes on the hour as you taste the blood
around your mouth,
Recalling the sighs and the couplings upon that floor.

There, mindless of your tread,
A goblet rolls, its gold long beaten down,
And lodged within, decked out in its own
        thread,
A spider climbs, performs both king and
        clown:
Cap of mute bells, and dark inverted
        crown.

Crack the archwizard's staff, impale his head upon it;
It splinters into the soil, and is fed by the slime o his
        corpse,
To burgeon as weeds that will poison the
        many-frontiered river,
Its yellow stench filling the chests of the people in the
        capitals:
Summers shall be autumns, middays shall be evenings,
With your victory flags to wrap you against the frost.

Where now my dynasty, so denied to him?
His was the interregnum begetting an epoch.

The mocking royal reflection in the cup:
The spider turns his sixty seconds round.
I occupied the tyrant's seat at the board
To show that anyone can claim his place
And freely sup,
Even as his power drains into the ground;
Alone among the guests, I had explored
Successive reigns of energy, or grace.

Raise the white palaces over the southern cities,
Parapeted platforms and squares where the dusk lies

DUNFERMLINE

        pink,
To become the theatre of guitars and kisses.

Surging of the crowds to the scabrous balcony,
As revolution opposes revolution:
Battle-dressed lovers place flowers in their rifles,
As the flickering lights mark the first shoots,
Tricolour ribbons over monochrome portraits:
While, guarding the mournful celebratory choir,
Stand simpering thugs awaiting their next hire.

PITTENCRIEFF PARK

Too many ghosts
Hovering by the pavilion; himself a ghost
Photographed, the laughing child: held by grandfather
Forenent the glasshouse: oh could he picture
His own descendants, to whom he'd be ghost indeed,
Not even a Hogmanay memory. But to him
Time breaks up and suspends its quivering droplets
On a leafless branch in the winter,
Droplets reflecting his lives in miniature
Absurd and imagined. By the gateway
The child of a child of his child shivers, awaiting,
Then suddenly smiles, and he marks well his own
           features
As she looks up, this girl kissing the lips
Of her earliest lover, as the year falls harsh to its death.

Oh could he fold to his heart the unlinkable,
But all's beyond his Proustian distortions

In this corner of Scotland; what's much more than
        himself : -

The eldritch legends and the grimy histories
Down the winding paths by the burn and under the
        bridges,
The perpetual carillon from the abbey tower.

Too many ghosts, for him to haunt alone,
Too many ghosts, the county's, and his own.

17. NO NEW STORIES: ROBERT HENRYSOUN AND ALEXANDER PUSHKIN

[Than upon him scho kest up baith hir ene –
And with ane blenk it come into his thocht
That he sumtime hir face befoir had sene.
Bot scho was in sic plye he knew hir nocht ...]
ROBERT HENRYSOUN, *The Testament of Cresseid*

1

The ballad 'Robene and Makyne' by Robert Henrysoun (c1436-c1503/4), schoolmaster at Dunfermline Abbey and medieval Scots makar, is a great performance piece. It requires two actors, male and female, to release the covert (or even overt) eroticism of the poem.

It's the comic counterpart to the same poet's darker masterpiece *The Testament of Cresseid*. The lines quoted above refer to Prince Troilus's last encounter with his former lover Cresseid, who had become a prostitute and leper. The scholar Matthew McDiarmid claimed Henrysoun as the greatest tragic poet between Dante and Shakespeare.

The basic plot of 'Robene and Makyne' is this: boy and girl meet; girl fancies boy; he isn't interested. Later, however, he decides that he fancies her after all, but as far as she's concerned,

The man that will nocht quhan he may
Sall haif nocht quhan he wald.

('The man that will not when he may / Shall have nothing
when he would.')

Tough.

Several centuries later, the great Russian poet Alexander
Pushkin wrote his verse novel *Eugene Onegin* (1833), which
is known to westerners mostly via Tchaikovsky's operatic
version. Pushkin, like many of his well-read compatriots at
the time, was familiar with certain aspects of Scottish literature
and thought. His aloof, dandified Eugene cultivates a western-
leaning cosmopolitanism: he is an avid reader of Adam Smith's
Wealth of Nations. Pushkin himself knew the work of Walter
Scott, and even translated the ballad 'The Twa Corbies' into
Russian. (Edwin Morgan later translated it back into Scots, but
that, as they say, is another story ...) However, there's no way
that Pushkin would have been aware of the medieval Scots
makars. Nevertheless, the plot of *Eugene Onegin* is essentially
that of 'Robene and Makyne'. Visiting provincial Russia, and
bored with its limitations, Onegin is introduced to the naïve,
sheltered Tatyana, who falls in love with him. Predictably he
rejects her and returns to his elegantly futile driftings across
Europe. In due course he returns to Russia and, attending a
lavish ball, he has sight of a beautiful princess: it's Tatyana,
transformed into a poised, sophisticated married lady. Now it
is Onegin's turn to make overtures to the woman he had once
dismissed; she confesses that she still loves him, but it's too
late. Onegin has no alternative but to shuffle off.

2

There are no new stories. The Scottish composer Ronald Stevenson (1928-2015) liked to quote, from the second part of Goethe's *Faust*, a dialogue between a clever-clever undergraduate and the much wiser devil Mephistopheles. The student arrogantly claims that his youth makes him an all-round innovator: 'The world was not, until I made it whole'. He earns this riposte from Mephistopheles: 'Go, my original, your glorious way! – How truth would irk you, if you really sought it: / For who can think of truth or trash to say / But someone in the ancient world has thought it?' (Philip Wayne's translation, Penguin, 1959).

'Originality', then, is overrated. The greatest writers possess the humility to recognise the classics of the past and to revisit them in their own work. This was the attitude of nineteenth-century Russians, who were eager to explore and inherit the cultures of the west. They would turn, for example, to Shakespeare, hence Ivan Turgenev's 'Prince Hamlet of the Shchigrovsky District' and 'A Lear of the Steppes'; Nikolai Leskov gave us his 'Lady Macbeth of the Mtsensk District' (again, that's better known to us in the form of Shostakovich's opera).

For once, at least, Goethe's worldly demon is in the right, and no practitioner in literature or the other arts should take the works of the past for granted, provided that they are available to him or her.

18. A TESTAMENT OF FIFE –
EIGHTH PART.
INVERKEITHING VIA
BENARTY TO KINCARDINE

Inverkeithing, Limekilns, Torryburn,
The southern townships on the southern shore,
Lumphinnans to Lochgelly and Lochore,
Benarty: that our folk are free to turn
To the deserved beauty of the kinrik's core.

Woodlands and lochside benches, playgrounds and
        trails,
Where howkers have yielded to hikers, canaries to
        dogs;
Owls now perch where coal was run on rails;
And whoever sweats here now, is one who jogs.

Here's Culross Abbey kirkyaird: what can save
Its bodies from oblivion altogether
Is the symbol of their trade, carved over their grave,
Rather than maudlin memory in pub blether.

Now we reckon how far we've come
From Ormiston, Newburgh and Mugdrum,

To Devilla Forest, where we come near
The county's counterpart frontier,

And at the last stop in Kincardine,
Dear reader, I must beg your pardon,

For now we part. Each Scots canton
Thrives by cultural comparison,

So I'm over the Forth for a raucle Fest
With the bookish workers of the west.

19. NOTES

2. A TESTAMENT OF FIFE – FIRST PART.
Mugdrum to Balcomie

'St Andrews, where the rush of water on stone [...]': This and subsequent stanzas refer to the chapter 'The Exhortations of Father Zossima' in Fyodor Dostoevsky's novel *The Brothers Karamazov:* 'My brother asked the birds to forgive him; that sounds senseless, but it is right; for all is like an ocean, all is flowing and blending; a touch in one place sets up movement at the other end of the earth.' (Constance Garnett's translation.)

Interestingly, that other giant of the nineteenth-century Russian novel, Lev Tolstoy, also takes up the image of the ocean, but in a context less ecological than moralistic: 'Men have made subdivisions for themselves in this eternally moving, unending, intermingled chaos of good and evil: they have traced imaginary lines on that ocean, and expect the ocean to divide itself accordingly, as if there were not millions of other subdivisions made from quite other points of view on another plane.' (From Tolstoy's short story 'Lucerne', in Aylmer Maude's translation.)

As regards **'another Russian's call'**, this refers to the former Soviet leader Mikhaïl Gorbachev who, shortly after the death of his wife Raïsa in 1999, made an appearance at a theatre and asked the actors to allow him to sing the poem 'Vykhozhu odin ya na dorogu' by Mikhaïl Lermontov (1814-41). Lermontov's Scottish ancestors are accepted to have been based in the area of St Andrews and Crail. My version of the poem appears here in Scots; please refer to the Glossary / Wordleet for definitions in English.

"Smoke, the unknowing of our evanescence": '"Smoke, smoke," [Litvinov] repeated several times: and it suddenly seemed to him that everything was smoke: everything – his own life, Russian life, everything human, especially everything Russian.' (Ivan Turgenev, *Smoke*; Natalie Duddington's translation.) However, the 'young Russian' of the present poem is, again, Mikhaïl Lermontov, whose ancestors the Learmonths inhabited Balcomie Castle between Crail and the county's easternmost point, Fife Ness.

Smoke and ocean …

'Why am I not that raven of the steppe': a translation of Lermontov's poem 'Zhelaniye' ('A Wish'). Here the poet imagines his ancestral Scotland, a country he never visited.

My version appeared as a kind of Greek chorus in my novel *Marie B.* (Ravenscraig Press, 2008), at a point where the heroine, the Ukrainian-French painter Marie Bashkirtseff, having visited her native land, contemplates her next move.

3. CLEAN PRIDE AND MUCKY PRIDE. Parochialism versus Provincialism

A longer version of this essay appeared in the first issue of the online magazine *The Pathhead Review* (Spring 2011).

4. A TESTAMENT OF FIFE – SECOND PART. Monimail to Craigtoun

'We remember Marianna Lines': Born in Atlanta, Georgia, and resident in Collessie, Fife, Marianna (1944-2018) was an artist and folklorist, well-known for her designs inspired by Pictish imagery.

'A family trip to Craigtoun Park': a personal reminiscence from September 1966. The park has since undergone extensive renovation, and the Italian Garden promises to become a more attractive feature than it was fifty-odd years ago. Nevertheless, I haven't grown out of my teenage craze for landscape-gardening features such as decorative structures (including follies, temples, belvederes, pagodas, fake ruins and so on), at their weirdest and most atmospheric.

5. BLEAK FERTILITY: ROBERT LOUIS STEVENSON AND FIFE.

A version of this essay appeared in *Platform*, a St Andrews University student magazine, in the autumn of 1983.

'Stevenson's uncle, another John Balfour [...] It was at Leven in 1871 that Louis met a workman [...]': See also the third paragraph of 'Herman Melville, Fife and *Moby-Dick*' later in this book.

6. A TESTAMENT OF FIFE – THIRD PART.
Cupar to Lower Largo

'Where a quarryman's son of Aberdeen': In the sequence 'Back-Green Odyssey' by Alastair Mackie (1925-95), the poet contemplates sea-voyaging as he sits in the garden of his Anstruther home: 'A herbour is a tension atween twa pulls / the beck o horizons and the rug o hame.' [A harbour is a tension between two pulls, the beckoning of horizons and the

TOM HUBBARD

tug of home.'] His *Collected Poems 1954-1994*, including his many translations, appeared posthumously from Two Ravens Press in 2012. The book was edited by Mackie's former pupil at Anstruther's Waid Academy, the writer Christopher Rush.

'Serpentine Walk to Lower Largo': during World War 2, Polish servicemen were based on the east coast of Scotland, where they remained consequent on the Stalinist takeover of their country and their marriages with local girls. My father's cousin became one of these wives. See the first story, 'Mrs Makarowski' in my book *Slavonic Dances* (Grace Notes Publications, 2017), though that is by no means based on our family situation and is entirely fictional.

7. HERMAN MELVILLE, FIFE AND *MOBY-DICK.*

This essay grew out of my lecture on *Moby-Dick* given at various universities in Scotland and the US between 1991 and 1999, as part of courses in American literature or in maritime fiction.

'To return to the area around Scoonie': see note to the essay 'Bleak Fertility' earlier in the present book, on Robert Louis Stevenson and Fife and his encounters with a workman in Leven.

'The Dunfermline writer David Thomson [...]': we can be grateful to the scholar Dr Jean Barclay for researching the 1897 serialisation of Thomson's novel *John Orrason: or the Adventures of a Social Castaway* in the *Dunfermline Press*. She prepared the text for book publication by Double Bridge Press, the imprint of Dunfermline Heritage Community

Projects. We're also indebted to the then head of publishing at DHCP, Clive Willcocks, and his team, for making the book available in 2010 (ISBN 978-0-9557244-1-1).

Dr Barclay's scholarly undertaking is comparable to the work of Dr William Donaldson, who likewise resurrected, during the 1980s and 1990s, two Victorian Scottish novels which had been previously published only in serial form. These were works by the Aberdeen writer William Alexander (1828-94), best-known for *Johnny Gibb of Gushetneuk* (1871), his only novel to appear in book form during his lifetime.

'Weirdly-shaped outcrops of rock': on the late Marianna Lines, see the above note to 'A Testament of Fife – Second Part'. The First Nations of Marianna's original homeland of America would use such outcrops as sites of worship of the Great Spirit. To white folks they appear to have possessed an ambience which at best was ominous and at worst sinister. In the short story 'Roger Malvin's Burial' by Melville's friend Nathaniel Hawthorne (1804-64), we read the following in the course of a description of a deep forest and the base of a rock where two men, wounded in battle and in danger of their lives, have been forced to rest: 'The mass of granite, rearing its smooth, flat surface fifteen or twenty feet above their heads, was not unlike a gigantic gravestone, upon which the veins seemed to form an inscription in forgotten characters.' My drawing represents the Bannet Stane (bonnet stone) on the western slope of West Lomond in Fife.

8. A TESTAMENT OF FIFE – FOURTH PART.
Methil to the Caves and Abandoned Pits

'G and S': Gilbert and Sullivan (but you maybe knew that already? Just in case).

'Butcher's Apron': the Union Jack.
'The silence of caves and pits': refers to the proximity of the Wemyss Caves, with their ancient Pictish carvings, to abandoned mine-shafts.

9. WALKIN IN FIFE: DUNCAN GLEN, MARKINCH AND POINTS NORTH.

A version of this essay appeared as the introduction to *Walking in Rural Fife in the 1950s and Noting Many Changes in 2007* (Akros Publications, 2007) by the late poet, publisher, editor and graphic designer Duncan Glen, who is the joint dedicatee of the present book. In his 2007 pamphlet, Glen included a selection of poems from his sequence 'Walkin in Fife' which first appeared in book form in the poet's collection *Realities Poems* (Akros, 1980). *Walking in Rural Fife* also includes photographs of Markinch, the Lomonds and their hinterland, by the poet himself and his daughter and son-in-law, Alison and Andrew Kelly.

Another selection from the 'Walkin in Fife' sequence appeared in Glen's *Collected Poems* (Akros, 2006).

10. A TESTAMENT OF FIFE – FIFTH PART.
Ravenscraig to Kirkcaldy

'Ravenscraig Elegy': this poem appears as the last piece in my pamphlet collection *The Nyaff* (Windfall Books, 2010). More on Duncan Glen: the poet's wife Margaret, who is central to the sequence 'Walkin in Fife', survived him by four years, dying of cancer in 2012. Akros Publications, one of Scotland's leading small poetry presses, was a husband-and-wife team effort; the sculptor Kenny Munro and I sought to recognise this in the form of a memorial stone to be sited in

Kirkcaldy's Ravenscraig Park near the Glen home in Lady Nairn Avenue. Duncan loved this park which includes a stretch of the Fife Coastal Path. Accordingly, in the spring of 2015, Kenny's work was unveiled at a short ceremony at the site, with readings from Duncan's poetry. An explanatory plaque is positioned adjacent to the stone, and includes biographical details of Duncan and Margaret, and it's our hope that walkers, attracted by Kenny's work, will go on to discover the legacy of this remarkable couple.

Kenny Munro, who lives in Kinghorn, is celebrated in the present book at the opening of 'A Testament of Fife – Sixth Part'.

'In a Kirkcaldy Warkin-Cless Airt': this poem appeared in my first pamphlet collection *Sax Sonnets in Scots* (Scots Glasnost, 1987) and was reprinted in *Four Fife Poets: Fower Brigs ti a Kinrik* (Aberdeen University Press, 1988). The poets were myself, William Hershaw, John Brewster and the late Harvey Holton.

'raiths': a raith is a quarter of a year, but there is also a pun on Raith, a bourgeois district of Kirkcaldy, and which is named after Raith House, an aristocratic pile sited imposingly atop a hill.

'store': the co-op.

Scots words, as always in the present book, are explained in the Glossary / Wordleet at the end.

12. THE DEVIL AND MICHAEL SCOT: a play.

This play tells the tale of the great polymath Michael Scot (c1175–c1235), associated with Balwearie Tower, west of Kirkcaldy, and the Borders (especially Melrose and the Eildon Hills). He was one of the leading intellectuals of medieval Europe, and is mentioned in Dante's *Inferno*. As a pioneer scientist he attracted accusations of black magic; the legends of his pact with the devil make him something of a Scottish Faust. In the list of Persons of the Drama, the names in brackets are of roughly equivalent characters in Goethe's *Faust*.

Indeed the play's narrative draws on a scenario devised by Samuel Taylor Coleridge for a Faust play in English; this is outlined in the poet's *Table Talk* for February 16, 1833. Coleridge did not pursue the project, but the material seemed to me to be too good to remain dormant.

I originally wrote a version in Scots between 1993 and 1995; at the time I was in receipt of a Scottish Arts Council Writer's Bursary which was geared specifically to the project. In a spirit of pragmatism, however, I also prepared the English version which is the title-piece of the present book; it enabled me to take the work to the USA during a visiting academic stint. Accordingly *The Devil and Michael Scot* was premièred as readers' theatre by the Black Swan Players in Asheville, North Carolina, during February 1997.

Extracts from the text have been published, variously in English and Scots, in the following publications: *Alba literaria* (ed. Marco Fazzini, Venice, 2001); *The Flechitorium* (Grace Notes Publications, 2017); *Lallans; Mither Ape* (a Scotsoun CD of my poems, 2019); *NorthWords; Scottish Faust* (Kettillonia, 2004); *Skinklin Star* (a Glasgow University postgraduates' broadsheet). A poem based on a shorter version of the story, 'The Testament of Michael Scot', was translated into French by Dominique Delmaire and performed as poetry theatre by Les Alpes Vagabondes, during the summer of 1993, in Gap.

My monograph *Michael Scot: Myth and Polymath* appeared from Akros Publications in 2006.

'A fog that hovered over that rough-carved throne: I was thinking of the 'Gothic' chair that is positioned at the head of a long wooden table, in one of the atmospheric side-rooms in Bannerman's pub in Edinburgh's Cowgate. The ambience had reminded me of the Auerbach's Keller scene in Goethe's *Faust.*

'Enough of blethering! The game's a bogy!': the phrase 'the game's a bogy' means, for Michael, 'That's it! It's time to move on from past mistakes and live anew!' 'Bogy' can also be spelt 'bogey' or 'bogie'. In his excitement Michael may be missing the full implications of the phrase: see Michael Munro's book *The Patter* (Birlinn, 2001), p. 20-21.

'the tree-like temple': e.g. the Goetheanum in Dornach, Canton of Basel, Switzerland.

'Where he misbuilt [...] She'll see right through.': an adaptation of lines from the closing scene of the opera *Doktor Faust* by Ferruccio Busoni.

The drawings for this play are based (1) on a gargoyle on a building in Alloa and (2) on a Gothic folly popularly if erroneously considered to be a tower belonging to Michael in the Balwearie area north of Kirkcaldy.

13. A TESTAMENT OF FIFE – SIXTH PART.
Kinghorn to Hawkcraig

'Kinghorn's man of ideas': Kenny Munro (b. 1954) is a well-known Scottish sculptor who lives in Kinghorn; see the notes on 'Ravenscraig Elegy', under 'A Testament of Fife – Fifth Part'.

The late **Ian McLeod** was a Scottish painter once associated with John Bellany and Sandy Moffat during the rebellious 1960s.

'Macbeth, staged on Inchcolm!': the play was indeed performed on the island, the ancient abbey serving as its décor. It was one of Richard Demarco's characteristically daring projects.

'Departure from the Island': this poem appeared in my pamphlet collection *Scottish Faust* (Kettillonia, 2004). I wrote it in North Carolina at a time when I was feeling homesick for the coast of Fife. Prospero is another Faustian figure.

14. FIFE'S FOLK CULTURE, PAST AND PRESENT: JOE CORRIE AND THE BOWHILL PLAYERS.

I drew the pencil portrait of Joe Corrie in 1988, to mark the thirtieth anniversary of his death; it was used for the cover of a special issue, that year, of the Fife literary magazine *Scrievins*. It was subsequently reproduced in *Lallans* magazine, to accompany an article on Corrie by William Hershaw. The drawing itself was exhibited in the Lochgelly Centre during the fiftieth anniversary events there. It's also reproduced on the website of the Joe Corrie symposium organised by St Andrews University in October 2018, and in Mike Quille's online magazine *Culture Matters* where the present essay was first published in September 2019.

15. HAUF A KILT IN KELTY.

'A year later, however, I was back in Hungary': see my preface to Stewart M. Macpherson's pamphlet, *Saint Margaret, Queen of Scotland; King David: a Sair Sanct* (Akros, 2007).

16. A TESTAMENT OF FIFE – SEVENTH PART.
Dunfermline

'The Prophecy of Banquo' first appeared in my pamphlet *Scottish Faust* (Kettillonia, 2004) as part of a series of poems, 'Scottish Poems for Shakespeare'. The late Sam Wanamaker had contacted me about my editing a possible multi-authored anthology with that title, but in spite of my efforts that collection didn't materialise. Instead, I wrote the series in memory of Sam.

'Pittencrieff Park': the accompanying drawing represents a scene in the park, but poetic license has been taken here. The last two lines of the poem are an echo of 'The Retour o Troilus' in my collection *Parapets and Labyrinths* (Grace Notes Publications, 2013).

17. NO NEW STORIES: ROBERT HENRYSOUN AND ALEXANDER PUSHKIN.

I was chairperson of the Robert Henrysoun Society from 2002 to 2005 and this essay is based on part of my address to the 2004 AGM of the Society.

20. WORDLEET / GLOSSARY

aa – all
ain – own
alow – below
anaa – as well, also
ane – one
apen – open
aroun – around
ava – at all
aw – all
aye – always; fir aye – forever
ayebydin – eternal
bade – lived, stayed, resided
bairnspiel – children's play
baith – both
baurs – bars
befoir – before
bield – to shelter
blae-like – bluish
blenk – instant (blink)
bletherin(g) – talking too much, talking nonsense
bruckle – brittle
buik-leired – book-learned
byde on – remain
cauld – cold
chaumer – chamber
clertie – clarty, messy, dirty, muddy
cranreuch – hoar-frost

cuid – could
dae – do
daurk – dark
deed – died
diamant – diamond
didnae – didn't
doun – down
dunts – blows, wounds, disappointments
Edinburry – Edinburgh (Fife pronunciation)
eldritch – weird, uncanny
emerant – emerald
ene – eyes
ettle – try, attempt
fae – from
fasht – troubled
fir aye – forever
foosty – pompously bombastic, stale, old-fashioned, uncool, naff
fly – crafty, devious; often applied to people from Fife, as in 'fly Fifer'
fowk – folk
frae – from
fremmit – strange, foreign, unfamiliar
fyke – fuss
gallimaufry – hodge-podge
gang – go
gars – compel
gin – if
girnin(g) – complaining, sometimes pettily
glister – glisten
goavin – staring stupidly
gowden – golden

gowk – fool, idiot
grun – ground
haar – thick, fog
hae – have
hairt – heart
hame – home
hauf – half
hert – heart
hichts – heights
hir(e) – her
hit's – it's
hotchin(g) – crowded
houk – dig
hunner – hundred
juist – just
kent – knew
kest – cast
kinrik – kingdom (Fife is often variously cited as 'the Kingdom of Fife' and 'the People's Republic of Fife)
lair – grave
lane, my – alone, i.e. I go alone
lang – long
leevin – living
leid – language, dialect, speech
mair – more
makar – poet
mebbe – maybe, perhaps
mony – many
muilderin – mouldering
muirland – moorland
nae – no, not

nocht - nothing

numpties – contemptible fools, feckin eedjits

ocht – anything

oors – ours

plye – plight

pyne – pain

quaitly – quietly, calmly

quate – quiet, calm

raith – (1) quarter of a year; (2) name of a district of
Kirkcaldy

raucle – bold, robust, with a hint of rough

reesle – rustle

roch – rough

routhie – abundant, profuse

sacrit – secret AND / OR sacred

sae – so

scho – she

schuil – school

sic – such

sin – since

smaa – small

smitch – stain, blemish, smudge

snowk – sniff out furtively

store – the co-op

stravaigin(g) – wandering, travelling

syle – soil

syne – since

tak – take

tasht – stained, blemished

than – then

thegither – together

thir – those

thocht – thought
thoosan – thousand
ti – to
tint – lost
toun – town
tuimness – emptiness
unkent – unknown
upby – up there
unco – uncanny, strange
wad – would
wark – work
warlock – a sinister and often supernatural creature
warsles – struggles, wrestles
wey – way
whit – what
yetts – gates
yird – earth
yit - yet

21. ABOUT THE AUTHOR

Tom Hubbard is a novelist, poet and former itinerant academic whose second novel, *The Lucky Charm of Major Bessop,* appeared from Grace Note Publications in 2014; readers are still working out the teasing clues in this 'grotesque mystery of Fife'. His other works of fiction are the novel *Marie B.* (Ravenscraig Press, 2008), based on the life of the late-nineteenth century painter Marie Bashkirtseff, and, more recently, *Slavonic Dances* (Grace Note, 2017), a set of three linked novellas based on the comic and tragic encounters of the Scottish characters with eastern and east-central Europe. His book-length collections of poetry are *The Chagall Winnocks* (2011), *Parapets and Labyrinths* (2013), and *The Flechitorium* (2017), all Scottish and European in their scope and also published by Grace Note. Tom was the first Librarian of the Scottish Poetry Library and went on to become a visiting university professor in France, Hungary and the USA. He has also worked as a researcher at Maynooth University in his ancestral Ireland. From 2000 to 2015 he edited the online Bibliography of Scottish Literature in Translation (BOSLIT); for this he conducted research in many mainland European countries. Between 2013 and 2016 he edited volumes of essays on Baudelaire, Flaubert and Henry James for Grey House of New York, and a three-volume annotated selection of the writings of Andrew Lang for Taylor & Francis. The pamphlet *Minoritie Status* (Tapsalteerie Press 2017) consists of Scots versions of the work of the Hungarian poet Győző Ferencz, and Tom has also worked on other translations of Hungarian poetry, as commissioned by Dr Zsuzsanna Varga of Glasgow University. In Dundee he recorded his Scots versions of European poetry for the CD *The Scots Leid in Europe,* released in June 2017 by Scotsoun (Scots Language Society / Scots Leid Associe).

More recently, he collaborated with Sheena Blackhall, Aberdeen's City Makar, on a pamphlet *From Gweedore to Skibbereen: Irish Poems, Ballads and Pieces* (Malfranteaux Concepts, 2019), and issued a CD of his poems in Scots, *Mither Ape* (Scotsoun SSCD, 2019), with the voices of Dorothy Lawrenson, Lisa Simmons, George T. Watt and himself.

In November 2015 he was elected an Honorary Member of the Széchenyi Academy of Letters and Arts, Budapest, and in April 2017 he became an Honorary Fellow of the Association of Scottish Literary Studies, which is administered at Glasgow University.

He lives in his native Kirkcaldy.

Printed in Poland
by Amazon Fulfillment
Poland Sp. z o.o., Wrocław

57079464R00094